The Bravehearts Toolbox

for Practitioners Working with Child Sexual Assault

Bravehearts inc.
Educate. Empower. Protect.

Nadine McKillop ▪ Carol Ronken ▪ Sam Vidler

www.
AUSTRALIANACADEMICPRESS
.com.au

First published in 2011
Australian Academic Press
32 Jeays Street
Bowen Hills Qld 4006
Australia
www.australianacademicpress.com.au

National Library of Australia Cataloguing-in-Publication entry:

Author:	McKillop, Nadine
Title:	The Bravehearts toolbox for practitioners working with sexual assault / Nadine McKillop, Carol Ronken, Sam Vidler.
Edition:	1st. edition
ISBN:	9781921513886 (pbk.) 9781921513893 (ebook)
Subjects:	Bravehearts. Child sexual abuse. Sexually abused children--Counseling of. Sexually abused teenagers--Counseling of. Sexually abused children--Care. Sexually abused teenagers--Care. Sexually abused children--Identification. Sexually abused teenagers--Identification
Other Authors/Contributors:	Ronken, Carol. Vidler, Sam.
Dewey Number:	362.76

Cover design by Maria Biaggini.

The artwork on the cover of this book was produced by a client of Bravehearts. Sara* (10) chose to title the canvas painting 'Playground of Emotions' and the original proudly hangs in the waiting room of our Springwood Counselling Service.
*Note: the client's name has been changed.

Testimonials

This how-to book facilitates education, empowerment, and protection by clinicians who will integrate all the practical information and activities into their repertoire to increase therapeutic outcomes. I heartily endorse this publication as a critical resource for anyone working with children or adolescents.

— Dr John Barletta, Clinical Psychologist.

Written in a clear and concise manner leaving the reader in no doubt regarding the insidious nature of this crime and the impact upon the victim. Thoughtfully constructed and clearly sensitive to the needs of victims, it presents a set of tools that will enable the practitioner to more confidently address issues surrounding child sexual assault, and has the capacity to serve as a valuable resource for all those who work in the area.

— Dr Lynne M. Baker , University of Queensland

What I believe sets this book apart from other such books created for professionals is the simple, matter of fact, no-nonsense language that conveys, with simple questions for reflection at the end of each chapter, the faith in all of us, that together with some reflection and awareness, we can, will and already have the experience and the know-how to help children, through their resilience and with the right healing and support, return to their lives and futures as happy, fulfilled individuals.

— Svava Brooks, Co-founder, VP of Blátt áfram, www.blattafram.is, and independent Instructor for Darkness to Light Stewards of Children Training, Evidence-based Child Sexual Abuse Prevention Training, www.darknesstolight.org

Clearly laid out with good background information on myths, facts and statistics, this book is an excellent guide on dealing with such problems with practical, therapy-based activities with clear directions to follow. Frequented by preferential phrases to use and which to avoid, all of which can help improve the consultation, as well as important reminders of how a simple phrase or question can impact any legal investigation. Highly recommended to any therapist who works with children: not just those who specifically work with known child sexual assault.

— Dr Dylan Wilson, Paediatrician.

A must have for mental health practitioners, teachers, school counsellors, medical practitioners, allied health practitioners and for those who are uncertain about their ability to respond effectively and take action accordingly when someone discloses child sexual assault. Beautifully put together and easy to read.

— Jan Bond, Clinical Counsellor

This book increases the reader's confidence in their ability to respond to and treat clients who have experienced child sexual assault by providing information and skills based on the authors' obvious expertise in the area. It is essential reading for those just starting out in the field, but is equally as useful to the more experienced clinician looking to reinforce and extend on their existing therapeutic skills.

— Shelli Hastings, Clinical Psychologist

About Bravehearts

Bravehearts Inc. is a national, registered charity whose members advocate support, dignity and respect for all survivors of child sexual assault. Bravehearts was founded in 1997 by Hetty Johnston in response to disclosures of child sexual assault in her own family. The Bravehearts team believe that the provision of effective support and care to children who have been sexually assaulted and their non-offending families, together with effective prevention, early intervention and increased community awareness will provide a fundamental cornerstone necessary to a healthy society.

Bravehearts is incredibly proud to have made an enormous difference, not only in providing otherwise non-existent professional services for children who have been sexually assaulted, but also in increasing public awareness of child sexual assault nationally to unprecedented levels. Equally important has been Bravehearts' role in motivating the proactive pursuit of child protection across a range of organisations, and legislative reform right across the nation.

Bravehearts' work

Bravehearts is unlike any other organisation and is uniquely positioned to deal with the effects of this crime because:

- Bravehearts deals exclusively and holistically with the issue of child sexual assault.
- Bravehearts has no religious affiliation (we take no position on religion, just as we take no position on age, gender, sexuality, culture, or economic circumstance).
- Bravehearts has a proven achievement record and is nationally acknowledged as a leading organisation in terms of dealing with child sexual assault.

Bravehearts provides direct services to many in need and at risk. The vital work carried out by Bravehearts in the community includes: providing direct services to children, young people and adults affected by child sexual assault; supporting families and carers; the development and provision of prevention programs and resources; advocating and lobbying for the voice of victims to be included in legislation and policy at all levels; promoting awareness about child sexual assault through training workshops and national campaigns such as White Balloon Day; and active involvement in research and policy development.

For more information about Bravehearts please go to www.bravehearts.org.au

Table of Contents

About the Authors

When developing this book the intention was to combine the expertise of both researchers and practitioners specialising in the area of child sexual assault to produce an innovative, evidence-based approach to working with children and young people affected by sexual assault. All three authors produced this book while employed by Bravehearts in research, practitioner and/or management roles.

Psychologist Nadine McKillop has extensive experience counselling both victims and offenders in Australia and abroad. Nadine's qualifications include a BA(Criminology and Criminal Justice), Bachelor of Behavioural Science and Bachelor of Psychology (Honours). For the past decade her practice has focused predominantly on child sexual assault. Nadine worked for Bravehearts as a psychologist until January 2010. Dedicated to continued research in this area, Nadine is a currently completing a Doctorate of Philosophy examining developmental and situational risk factors associated with the onset of child sexual assault, with a focus on informing primary prevention initiatives.

Carol Ronken worked as a researcher and Associate Lecturer at Griffith University in the School of Criminology and Criminal Justice before joining Bravehearts in early 2003. With a BA(Psych) and Masters in Social Research, Carol is the Research Manager for Bravehearts and is passionate about ensuring the organisation's active involvement in research, policy and legislative development that aims to prevent, respond to, and ultimately reduce the incidence of child sexual assault in the community.

Sam Vidler is a qualified counsellor who has been supporting children and families affected by sexual assault for several years. Sam's qualifications include a Bachelor of Arts and Graduate Diploma in Counselling. She is currently undertaking a postgraduate degree in psychology. In addition to working therapeutically with children, young people and parents, Sam was employed as Bravehearts' Therapeutic Services Manager until November 2010.

Acknowledgments

The techniques mentioned in this book have been reproduced from the internal resource, *Bravehearts Inc. Counsellors Toolbox*. We take this opportunity to thank psychologist Katie Boast for her contribution to the conception of a practitioner's toolbox for working with children affected by sexual assault, and the collation of techniques contained within it, during her time as Head of Counselling at Bravehearts. The expertise and contributions made by Katie and the Bravehearts counselling team members, past and present, have been invaluable to the development of Bravehearts' specialist approach to child sexual assault, and to the development of this book.

The authors would like to also acknowledge Bravehearts' Founder and Executive Director, Hetty Johnston, who initially proposed the idea of this book, with the infamous words: 'I was thinking that we should …' Hetty's determination and passion for ensuring that children and young people who have been sexually assaulted are not forgotten and are afforded every possible support has been the foundation of the work of the therapeutic and support team at Bravehearts. Through all the controversy and media attention, Hetty has remained focused on one important goal — protecting the most innocent members of our community.

How to Use This Book

Who is this book for?

As the incidence of child sexual assault continues to grow in today's society, so too does the demand for specialised counselling services. While Bravehearts has a dedicated, specialised therapeutic team based in South East Queensland, this service simply cannot meet the demand for therapeutic intervention that exists around Australia and indeed the world.

The Bravehearts therapeutic team often receive enquiries from practitioners who feel unsure about how to proceed following a client's disclosure that they have experienced sexual assault. They often lack confidence in how to best respond appropriately to such a disclosure, as they do not wish to re-traumatise their client, nor contaminate any possible legal proceedings. They are often uncertain about their reporting obligations and the legal ramifications following their actions. Further, they are often unsure as to how to proceed with counselling once sexual assault is indicated. Simply, they feel they do not have the confidence or tools to counsel children and young people affected by sexual assault.

Children and adolescents may attend counselling for any number of reasons: anger management, self-esteem issues, eating disorders, bullying, and so on. Often, sexual assault is masked by these presentations, and it is not until a counsellor or therapist has spent many sessions engaging the young person and building rapport and trust that the client feels comfortable enough to disclose sexual assault (Jensen, Gulbrandsen, Mossige, Reichelt, & Tjersland, 2005).

Bravehearts recommend that if a therapeutic relationship has already been established with a child or young person, and they have chosen you to disclose their experience of sexual assault to, where possible, it is preferable to continue working with your client. By referring them to another therapist or agency following a disclosure, it is possible that, due to the inhibiting disclosure effects of child sexual assault (Goodman-Brown, Edelstein, Goodman, Jones, & Gordon, 2003; Paine & Hansen, 2002) the child may disengage from counselling altogether and it may be years before they feel able to trust someone enough to disclose again, if at all. More importantly, research has identified the importance of the therapist's response to disclosure for both the healing and potential secondary victimisation of clients (Denov, 2003).

With this is mind, this book is an essential guide for general counsellors, school counsellors, psychologists, youth workers, chaplains, mental health practitioners and other allied health professionals, to provide them with the necessary information and skills to support children and young people affected by sexual assault. This book's purpose is to build the confidence of these frontline workers and to reassure them that they do in fact possess the necessary skills to continue to work with their client once the issue of sexual assault has been raised. This book is an introduction to the specialised practice of counselling children and young people affected by sexual assault, rather than an exhaustive resource. Further reading and practitioner training is actively encouraged to complement learnings from this resource.

What will this book help you achieve?

This book is both process-oriented and skills-based and provides specific information regarding:

- understanding the nature of child sexual assault
- effective responses to disclosures of sexual assault within the therapeutic environment
- helping parents to respond appropriately and effectively to disclosures, and to understand behaviours and emotions often associated with child sexual assault
- strengthening your therapeutic approach to children affected by sexual assault
- effective therapeutic interventions with children who have experienced sexual assault
- understanding the principles behind psycho-educational tools to teach personal safety messages to children
- understanding the toll on the therapist when working in the area of child sexual assault and identifying key self-care and organisational-care strategies to minimise this effect
- tailoring therapeutic responses to your workplace setting.

This book provides readers with comprehensive information along with some basic therapeutic skills on how to respond to children and young people who have experienced sexual assault. It is Bravehearts' experience that children in particular are not usually comfortable sitting face-to-face for an hour talking about their feelings and emotions. Instead, activities such as games and craft projects are effective tools for rapport building and to provide time for counsellors and clients to talk and build trust.

While this book is process rather than theory based, the techniques outlined draw on many different theoretical modalities, including cognitive-behavioural therapy, expressive therapy and person-centred therapy. Anecdotal evidence from Bravehearts' therapists indicate that these strategies have proven beneficial in enhancing child-parent attachment, building the client's self-esteem and addressing other issues such as bullying and grief and loss.

Bravehearts counselling is predominantly person-centred. To a large extent the child directs what happens within the session. Person-centred therapy provides children with a sense of control and empowerment that can be missing in their everyday life if they have been sexually assaulted. Expressive and play therapy is also used, incorporating activities such as painting, drawing and sandtray. These creative therapies provide children with an age appropriate medium to safely and comfortably explore and express their emotions (Bratton, Ray, Rhine, & Jones, 2005; Gil, 1991; O'Connor & Braverman, 1997). They are non-directive and tailored to meet the child's maturational needs.

How to use this book

This book was designed to provide readers with some introductory therapeutic tools that may be used or adapted for use in individual workplace settings, making it an ideal companion for newly qualified practitioners, as well as more experienced practitioners wanting to extend their repertoire of counselling skills.

The techniques and strategies outlined must be considered as individual components that form part of the overall process of counselling. As you are working with children who have experienced trauma, be aware that each technique only addresses one aspect of your overall case plan. They must be utilised in a holistic manner, while normalising the child's emotional and psychological response to sexual assault and allowing them to explore and express their associated feelings in a safe way — for example, by using expressive therapies such as sandtray, painting, drawing and play.

It must be emphasised that to use an individual technique in isolation for this client group may have a detrimental effect, as on their own they are too simplistic a response for a traumatised child. However, as part of a holistic therapeutic response, that focuses on healing the underlying feelings, we have found that these strategies can empower the child, resulting in an increased sense of mastery over how they think, behave, feel, and ultimately heal.

You will find a set of review questions at the end of each chapter. These have been designed as a self-reflection and evaluation tool and we recommend you use them to assess your knowledge and understanding of the material covered. While this may be completed individually, it also makes an ideal resource for continued professional development and may be included as part of your workplace professional development program.

We hope that you find this book useful to your professional development. Bravehearts' therapeutic team would be happy to respond to any questions about the material provided in this book. A feedback form has also been included on the last page.

Nadine McKillop, BA(CCJ), BBSc(Psych) (Hons)
Carol Ronken, BA(Psych), MAppSoc(Research)
Sam Vidler, BA, Grad Dip Couns

Definitions

Child

A child is any person who has not yet reached the age of 18 (consistent with the United Nations Convention on the Rights of the Child).

Child protection

A broad term used to describe philosophies, policies, standards, guidelines and procedures to protect children from both intentional and unintentional harm. In the current context, it particularly applies to the duty of organisations and individuals associated with those organisations towards children in their care.

Child protection authorities

Term used to describe the various state and territory government bodies given the authority to provide for the protection of children.

Child sexual assault

Child sexual assault includes any act of inappropriately exposing or subjecting a child, under the age of 18, to sexual activity, contact or behaviour by an adult or by another child, for the purpose of gratification (sexual or otherwise).

Examples of child sexual assault include:

- fondling
- rape (includes digital and use of objects)
- indecent touching
- exposing a child to sexual acts
- exposing a child to pornography
- making a child look at another child or adult's genitals
- masturbation
- oral sexual acts
- exposure
- any sexual interactions with a child.

Indicators may include:

- fear of being hurt during nappy changing or dressing
- loss of concentration
- development of eating disorders
- fear of being alone with a particular person
- sexual themes in artwork, stories, play etc.
- showing a knowledge of sexual behaviour beyond their years
- bedwetting or soiling after being toilet trained
- 'acting out' or 'acting in' behaviours
- self-harming
- problems with friends and/or schoolwork
- vaginal, penile or anal soreness, discharge or bleeding.

Emotional abuse

Emotional abuse involves denigrating a child and excessive or unreasonable parental demands that place expectations on children beyond their capabilities.

Examples of emotional abuse include:

- continued verbal abuse
- put-downs
- rejections
- isolation
- threats
- persistent teasing
- ignoring or passive rejection
- withholding praise or affection.

Indicators may include:

- lack of self-esteem
- habit disorders (such as thumb sucking, biting, rocking)
- learning problems

- extremes in behaviour
- destructive behaviour to self or others
- inappropriately seeking attention and/or affection
- excessive compliance
- extreme passivity or aggression
- very demanding or alternatively very undemanding
- conduct disorders (such as withdrawal or antisocial behaviours).

Neglect

Neglect is the failure to provide a child with the basic necessities of life.

Examples of child neglect include:

- failure to provide adequate food and nutrition
- failure to provide shelter
- lack of emotional security
- neglect of medical and dental care
- inadequate supervision needed for the development of the child

Indicators may include:

- frequent hunger
- malnutrition
- poor hygiene
- inappropriate clothing
- left unsupervised for long periods
- medical needs not attended to
- stealing food
- staying at school outside school hours
- often being tired, falling asleep in class
- using alcohol or other drugs.

Physical abuse

Physical abuse occurs when a child suffers or is likely to suffer significant harm or injury inflicted by a child's parent, caregiver or other person in the child's life. The injury may be inflicted intentionally or may be the inadvertent consequence of physical punishment or physically aggressive treatment of a child.

Physical abuse can include:

- beatings
- shaking
- burning
- biting
- pinching
- poisoning
- smothering
- strangling
- Munchausen's syndrome by proxy

Indicators may include:

- neurological trauma (such as shaken infant syndrome)
- head or internal injuries
- wearing long-sleeved clothes on hot days
- demonstrating fear of parent/caregiver
- becoming fearful when other children cry or shout
- being excessively friendly to strangers
- being passive and compliant
- developmental problems
- displaying aggressive behaviour
- not getting on well with peers
- physical indicators such as bruises, fractures or burns.
- extremes in behaviour.

Chapter 1

The Nature of Child Sexual Assault

The aim of this chapter is to provide practitioners with an increased understanding of the nature of child sexual assault in order to improve their therapeutic response. As child sexual assault remains such a taboo issue in society, it is imperative that we attempt to debunk the myths and empower therapists by providing them with accurate information. This in turn will allow professionals to better support and empower their clients.

Chapter overview

1. Defining the problem.
2. Defining child sexual assault.
3. Offenders and grooming.
4. The silence surrounding child sexual assault.
5. Signs and indicators.
6. Impact and effects.
7. Myths, facts and statistics.

Upon completion of this chapter it is intended that you:

1. have an understanding of what constitutes child sexual assault, including the myths and facts around this issue
2. have an increased knowledge of offenders and their patterns of behaviour
3. feel more confident in identifying the signs and indicators of sexual assault in clients
4. have an increased understanding of the short- and long-term impact and effects of child sexual assault.

Defining the problem

Child sexual assault is a hidden but significant problem in every community in Australia. Every year in Australia thousands of cases of sexual assault of children are reported to police and child protection authorities. Research suggests that around one in five children will be sexually assaulted before the age of 18 (see Spatz-Widon, 1993; Finkelhor, 1994; Goldman & Padayachi, 1997; James, 2000; Queensland Crime Commission, 2000). Sexual assault includes a continuum of offending behaviours. Based on a review of research conducted on child sex assault cases over an 8-year period, researchers estimated that between 5% and 10% of girls and up to 5% of boys are exposed to penetrative sexual abuse, and up to three times this number are exposed to any type of sexual assault (Gilbert, Spatz-Widom, Browne, Fergusson, Webb & Janson, 2009).

The most vulnerable ages for children to be exposed to sexual assault appears to be between three and eight years of age (Beitchman, Zucker, Hood, DaCosta, & Akaman, 1991; Browne & Lynch, 1994); while the Australian Bureau of Statistics report that 25% of victims of 'all' sexual assaults reported are aged between 10 and 14 (Australian Bureau of Statistics, 2009). Less than one in ten of these children will tell someone about the assault (Abdulrehman & De Luca, 2001; Alaggia, 2005; Jozon & Linbad, 2004; Orsoli, Kia-Keating & Grossman, 2008).

Research clearly shows that individuals who are sexually assaulted as children are far more likely to experience psychological problems, often lasting into adulthood, including: post-traumatic stress disorder, depression, substance abuse and relationship problems (Spataro, Mullen, Burgess, Wells, & Mos, 2004). Child sexual assault does not discriminate along lines of region, race, creed, socioeconomic status or gender; it crosses all boundaries to impact every community and every person in Australia.

Defining child sexual assault

Traditionally, child sexual assault has been 'lumped in the same pot' as child abuse and neglect. However, while all forms of abuse and assault are harmful to children it is important to take child sexual assault out of the 'pot' as the dynamics are fundamentally different. Recognising these differences and the varying ways necessary to respond to child sexual assault will enable this crime to be effectively addressed and prevented. Some of the important differences include:

- Acts of *child abuse and neglect* are generally unplanned, re-active and are generally aligned with socioeconomic and/or family dysfunction issues and are comparatively predominant in areas of social disadvantage.

Sexual assaults against children are almost always pre-meditated, involving predatory acts of grooming, manipulation, self-gratification and exploitation, and occur widely across the various socioeconomic areas.

- *Child abuse and neglect* more commonly involve the infliction of pain, violence and aggressive force.

  Child sexual assault more commonly involves manipulation, intimidation and inappropriate contact.

- *Child abuse and neglect* are perpetrated by a parent or primary caregiver in an estimated 90% of cases.

  Child sexual assault is generally perpetrated by a male and more likely to be perpetrated by someone known to the child or their family (research varies but commonly finds between 70% and 90% of the time; National Child Protection Clearinghouse, 2005). Of those offenders known to the child most commonly the offender is not living with the child (Kogan, 2004).

- *Child abuse and neglect* offences are almost always intra-familial.

  Child sex assault offences are commonly extra-familial as well as intra-familial.

Every state and territory has laws that prohibit sexual conduct with children and adolescents. Although these laws vary in details from state to state, they agree for the most part on what constitutes behaviour that is sexually exploitative. Broadly defined, child sexual assault includes:

> *Any act of inappropriately exposing or subjecting a child under the age of 18 to sexual activity, contact or behaviour by an adult or by another child for the purpose of gratification (sexual or otherwise).*

Often people think that child sexual assault refers only to rape. However, many survivors of child sexual assault may not experience penetrative offences such as rape. Instead they may experience a wide range of acts including genital exposure, fondling, forced touching, inappropriate kissing, oral sex, or exposure to pornography.

Some examples of behaviours that constitute the sexual assault of children include:

- Elizabeth is 10. Her father comes into her room when she is sleeping and pulls her nightgown up so that he can rub her genital area with his hands.
- Tim is three. His mother keeps him in her bed and masturbates him until he has an erection.

- Steve and his friend Ben are invited to play with their neighbour's Playstation. While playing, the neighbour suggests that the boys have a naked wrestling match while he takes pictures of them.
- Andrea is thinking about running away from home; her mother's boyfriend tries to kiss her while her mother is at work.
- Sally's teacher asks her to stay after class. While he is talking to her, he puts his arm around her and starts fondling her breast.
- Simon's football coach e-mails him pornographic stories involving men and young boys.
- Carl is 15. He babysits for his six-year-old niece. He gets into bed with her and makes her rub his penis.
- Tom's stepmother insists on giving him a bath, even though he is 10. She takes off her clothes and gets into the tub with him.

These are a few of the hundreds of examples of sexually exploitative behaviour. In each, we see a person who is taking advantage of someone younger and in a position of less power than they are.

As identified in these examples, offenders, while most often male, can sometimes be female; they may select a victim of the same sex or of the opposite sex; and they may be a family member, a friend or an acquaintance. Sometimes the offender may also be a minor.

Offenders and grooming

Views that children are at risk predominately from strangers have inhibited knowledge that most sexual assault of children occurs at the hands of someone the child knows, trusts and often loves.

We now know the people who most commonly sexually assault children are usually family members or individuals close to the family or child. Research shows that between 70–90% of the time, the sexual assault involves an offender who is known and trusted by the child (National Child Protection Clearinghouse, 2005). Strangers do indeed molest children. However, most of the time, the offender is not the 'bogeyman' hiding in the bushes. It is instead a parent, step-parent, sibling, grandparent, uncle, aunt, cousin, neighbour, family friend, teacher, member of the clergy, or someone else who is known to the child or their family.

Data from a sample of more than 500 clients attending therapy at Bravehearts Inc over a five-year period indicated that approximately 97% of offenders were known to the victim. Specifically, 37% of offenders were a parent or parental figure living in the child's primary or secondary residence, 31% were other family members, and 29% were known to the child and their family outside the home. Only 3% were strangers. These figures are consistent with existing research showing the majority of offenders to be either related to or closely affiliated with the child (Kogan, 2004).

As previously mentioned, despite impressions gained from media reports of sexual crimes, child sexual assault is most often not violent. Usually it involves a process of grooming and contrived compliance based on trickery, manipulation and secrecy with a child to whom the offender often has a close relationship (Smallbone & Wortley, 2000). Understanding these offending components, it becomes clearer how easily children can become coerced into silence, or indeed made to feel some responsibility for the offence.

In order to effectively prevent the sexual assault of children, it is essential that practitioners and the community understand offending behaviours and patterns. Understanding the processes of grooming and offending, helps in the recognition of the dynamics that impact on the children and young people you work with.

There are many terminologies used to describe child sex offenders and offences, including:

- **Child molesters:** generally defines people who sexually offend against children or young people.
- **Paedophilia:** defines people who have a sexual preference and/or attraction to pre-pubescent children.
- **Hebephilia:** defines the homosexual attraction of adult males to immediately post-pubertal boys.
- **Korephilia:** defines the homosexual attraction of adult females for young girls.
- **Incest:** commonly refers to child sexual assault perpetrated by a family member.

Defining who is an offender and who is likely to sexually offend against a child is complex. There is no 'simple' or single profile of a child sex offender. Child sex offenders do not adhere to a particular stereotype. Offenders come from all walks of life, all family types and all ages.

In trying to understand who offenders are it is important to note that there are two main categories of offenders (Lanning, 2001):

- **Situational offenders** are individuals who do not have a 'true' sexual preference for children, but sexually offend against children for varied and complex reasons. The situational offender usually has fewer numbers of victims.

- **Preferential** offenders have a definite sexual preference for children generally. Their sexual fantasies focus on children. These offenders tend to have higher numbers of victims.

Finkelhor (1984) has developed what is termed the 'four preconditions of sex abuse', which provides a model for understanding how the sexual assault of children occurs. The first precondition is the presence of an individual who has the motivation to sexually assault children. This motivation contains three components (any of which may be present but not all of which are required): emotional congruence, sexual arousal and blockage (an individual's inability to have a normal sexual relationship). Experience as a sexually assaulted child is a common feature leading to emotional congruence.

The second precondition is what Finkelhor (1984) terms internal inhibitors. Most individuals have internal inhibition of any intermittent desires to be sexually involved with children. When these internal inhibitors are absent, there is a greater likelihood of an abusive event. According to Finkelhor (1984) alcohol and drugs are the two most common destroyers of internal inhibitors.

The third precondition for child sexual assault is the overcoming of external inhibitors. In families the major external inhibitor is the presence of a protective parent. If the parent is not present or not protective then an individual with a motivation to sexually assault and no internal inhibitors finds the approach to a child easier.

The fourth precondition for child sexual assault is the breakdown of the child's resistance. Resistance may be taught either by parents or through education programs and include the empowerment and build up of resiliency and protective factors within the child and the child's environment. Overcoming external inhibitors and the resistance of a child are very much the intention of the grooming process.

Child sex offenders use a variety of tricks to 'groom' children or adolescents and often their primary caregivers. Common grooming techniques reported by offenders include (Leclerc, Proulx, & McKibben, 2005):

Building the child's trust: Using presents, special attention, treats, spending time together and playing games with non-sexual physical contact.

Favouritism: The offender treats the child as an adult; treating them differently and making them feel like a unique friend.

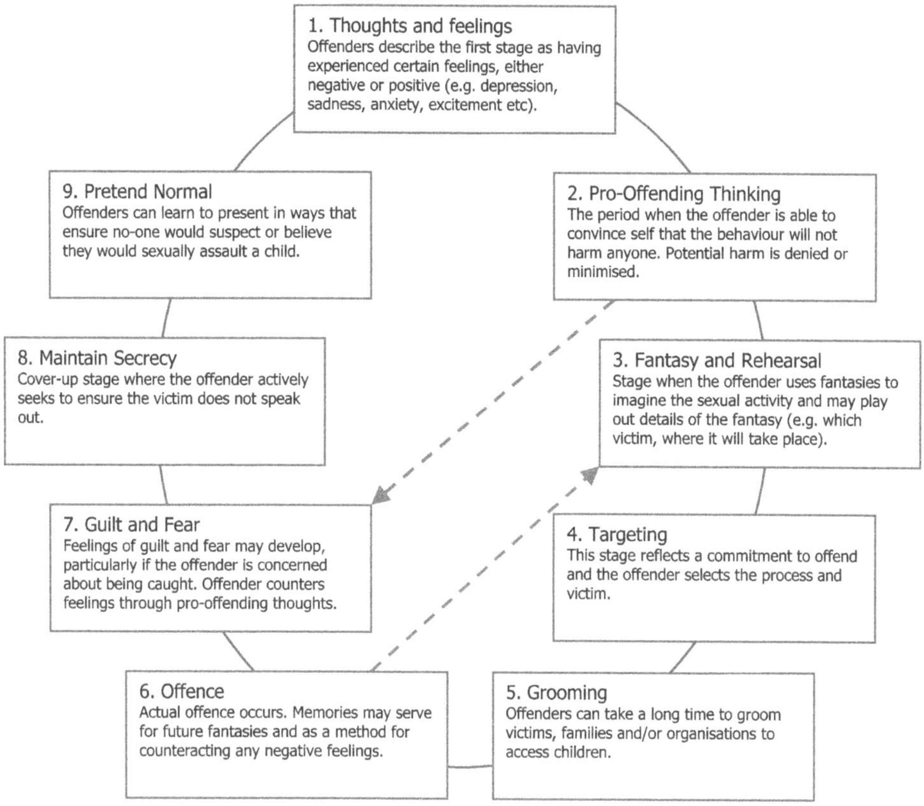

FIGURE 1

The sexual offending cycle.

Note: Adapted from the Core Sex Offender Management and Intervention Program, Victoria 2001.

Gaining the trust of the child's carer/s: Careful to be 'seen' as a close, caring and reliable relative or friend of the family.

Isolation (from family, friends): To ensure secrecy and lessen chances of disclosure or belief.

Intimidation and secrecy: The offender may use coercion — for example, threatening looks and body language, glares, stalking, and rules of secrecy.

'Testing the waters' or boundary violation: 'Innocent' touching, gradually developing into 'accidental' sexual contact.

Shaping the child's perceptions: The child is often confused as to what is acceptable and can take on self-blame for the situation, as his/her viewpoint can become totally distorted.

It is widely acknowledged that people who sexually assault children engage in a cyclical pattern of behaviour. While there are variations among sex offenders in how they operate, the cycle illustrated in Figure 1 on page 15 depicts a fairly typical pattern for child sex offenders. It is worth noting that this cycle would differ for situational (non-preferential) offenders, as well as for juvenile and female offenders.

The silence surrounding child sexual assault

The perpetration of child sexual assault relies heavily on silencing the victim; in order to keep offending, perpetrators need secrecy. Offenders usually put a great deal of effort into ensuring that a child remains silent. Apart from promises, threats and bribes, offenders also take advantage of the child's powerlessness by presenting a distorted or false view of what is happening. Some of the ways offenders 'trick' children into secrecy include convincing the child that:

- they are somehow responsible
- others will blame them
- they will be punished
- they will be to blame if the offender goes to jail
- they will be to blame if the family breaks up
- they will be to blame if others in the family are upset
- they are bad in some way and this is why the assault happened in the first place
- they will not be 'special' anymore; and/or
- no one would believe them if they told.

In childhood, the main factors influencing non-disclosure to family and friends are: when the offender is known to the child (Smith et al., 2000), when the offender is a family member (Crisma, Bascelli, Paci & Romito, 2004), or when the child perceives there may be more negative outcomes (e.g., not being believed, family break-up), than positive outcomes (e.g., the abuse stops, safety; Jensen et al., 2005).

One of the most commonly expressed reasons for not disclosing child sexual assault is a fear of not being believed (Jensen et al., 2005). Both children and adults report that this fear of non-belief is a major barrier to them disclosing to either trusted others or support services (Crisma et al., 2004).

In fact, such is the pervasive nature of this fear of disbelief, that even if a child has one or more supportive parents this does not necessarily increase their chances of disclosing their abuse history. In the common circumstance, where the abuse is from a parental figure, loved family member, or trusted family friend the perceived likelihood of belief of the child is also severely compromised (Alaggia &

Kirshenbaum, 2005). It is so often tough for anyone to disclose sexual assault. For children who do not have the language or the understanding of what has happened, it can be even more difficult. Some of the difficulties they face are listed below:

- They often feel it is their fault because they let it happen.
- They feel guilty about their body's natural reaction to sexual activity (even though this is beyond their control).
- They feel disclosure may cause family problems or breakdowns.
- The offender may be someone the child/young person heavily relies on.
- They fear they will be blamed, punished or not believed.
- They fear they will be taken away from their homes and their families if they speak out; and/or they fear disclosure will cause harm to someone or something they love and care for, such as family members or pets.

Signs and indicators

While children often lack the cognitive capacity and the words to describe sexual assault, finding it exceptionally difficult to disclose, they may try to subtly open the conversation by asking 'Do you like so and so?... I don't' or 'I've got a secret'. Unfortunately, the more severe the degree of offending the less likely it is that the child/young person will disclose (Paine & Hansen, 2002). This is why it is important for us as parents, carers, teachers, child protection workers, counsellors, and so on, to be vigilant for indicators of sexual assault.

There are a number of physical and behavioural symptoms that could be viewed as 'red flags' — a sign that something may be worrying the child. It should not be automatically assumed that a red flag means harm is occurring; talking to the child may reveal something quite innocent. It is important, however, not to dismiss significant changes in behaviour, fears or physical symptoms.

Common indicators of child sexual assault include:

- loss of concentration
- development of eating disorders
- fear of being alone with a particular person
- sexual themes in artwork, stories, play and so forth
- showing a knowledge of sexual behaviour beyond their years
- bedwetting or soiling after being toilet trained
- fear of being hurt during nappy change or dressing

- 'acting out' behaviours; for example, aggression, destructive behaviours, truanting behaviour
- 'acting in' behaviours; for example, withdrawal from friends, depression
- self-harming
- vaginal, penile or anal soreness, discharge or bleeding
- problems with friends and schoolwork
- vague symptoms of illness such as headache or tummy ache
- bruises, bite-marks or other injuries to breasts, buttocks, lower abdomen
- inappropriate displays of affection or sexualised play
- over-attention to adults of a particular sex.

Impact and effects

Children and adolescents who have been sexually assaulted can suffer a range of psychological and behavioural problems, from mild to severe, in both the short- and long-term.

The initial or short-term effects of sexual assault usually occur within two years of the termination of the assault (Bhave & Mashankar, 2006). These effects vary depending upon the circumstances of the offending, the child's developmental stage, whether or not they have disclosed, and the response to any attempts to disclose (Elliott & Carnes, 2001). Typical presentations at Bravehearts may include regressive behaviours, sleep disturbances, eating problems, behaviour, and/or performance problems at school and non-participation in school and social activities.

The negative effects of child sexual assault can affect the survivor for many years and into adulthood and include depression and self-destructive behaviours (Beitchman et al., 1992; Briere & Elliott, 1994). Many survivors also encounter problems in their adult relationships and in their adult sexual functioning.

Re-victimisation is also a common phenomenon among people harmed as children. Research has shown that child sexual assault survivors are more likely to be the victims of rape or to be involved in physically abusive relationships as adults (Beitchman et al., 1992; Briere & Elliott, 1994).

Despite all this, it is important to understand that the impacts and effects of child sexual assault can be reduced. Many survivors are able to live perfectly happy and secure lives. Children and adults who are supported and believed when they speak out are less likely to endure long-term negative impacts (Elliott & Carnes, 2001;

Wyatt & Mickey, 1987). The response of others to disclosed or suspected harm is a crucial factor.

Some of the common impacts and effects of child sexual assault seen in children and young people include:

- psychosomatic responses
- psychiatric disorders
- long-lasting emotional problems
- youth suicide
- regression
- sleeping and eating disorders
- lack of self-esteem
- nightmares
- self-harming/mutilation
- self-hatred
- promiscuous behaviour
- aggression
- behavioural changes.

A wide variety of effects that can be seen in the long-term include:

- the development of violent behaviour
- the development of criminal behaviour
- long-term psychiatric problems
- suicide
- posttraumatic stress
- sexual difficulties
- inability to form lasting relationships
- a serious lack of self-confidence
- marital problems
- poor parenting skills
- alcohol and substance misuse.

Myths, facts and statistics

Myths are often used to explain the unexplainable, to make sense out of things that make no sense. Sometimes people use myths to protect themselves from painful realities.

There are a number of myths and fallacies that surround the issue of child sexual assault because the reality of the problem is incomprehensible and frightening to many. These myths effect appropriate responses not only from individuals and the general community, but also can influence responses from the child protection and justice systems, as well as counselling and support services. Examples of some of the common myths and misinformation that surround this issue are discussed below.

Myth # 1

Sex offenders are strangers and just dirty old men.

Reality

Children are often warned not to talk to strangers in the hope that this will protect them from child sexual assault. Statistics suggest that around 90% of sexual assault is perpetrated by someone known to the child and/or their family (National Child Protection Clearinghouse, 2005). Rather than attacking from the bushes, the sexual offender uses his position and relationship with a child to control and manipulate.

Sex offenders are both male and female, all ages and from all walks of life. In fact, statistics show that the average age of sex offenders is 36 years of age (Hanson et al., 2002).

Myth # 2

Children 'invite' sexual assault by being or acting seductive.

Reality

The child is never at fault in sexual assault cases. The myth of the seductive child is a particularly cruel one. It implies that the child is responsible for the adult's behaviour.

Children sometimes act in a 'sexy' way because they have learnt that this kind of behaviour will get them attention. They want and need affection and attention from the adults in their world. They may emulate adult behaviour to get that attention, but no girl or boy wants to be sexually assaulted. Adults have power over children, and they must not manipulate this power.

Myth # 3

Child sexual assault is rare.

Reality

Around one in three girls and one in six boys will be sexually victimised by the age of 18 (Spatz-Widom, 1993). No one knows the exact number of victims of childhood sexual assault. Because the injuries in sexual assault are primarily emotional rather than physical, it is less likely that someone other than the victim will be aware of the assaults. Unless the victim tells someone, the sexual assault will not be reported and the victim may continue to be victimised.

Myth # 4

Child sexual assault is not harmful to children.

Reality

Studies show that sexual assault has many harmful effects on children. Survivors often need help and support to overcome these effects. Sexual assault of children often causes long-lasting emotional problems. Young victims often experience sleep problems, nightmares, nervous reactions, learning difficulties, depression, loss of self-esteem, behavioural difficulties, problems with peers, and the list goes on. A lot of children are frightened, especially when they have been threatened; many are confused, because they might enjoy some aspects of the relationship and may feel guilty about it, or they are too scared to tell anyone.

Not all victims experience all of these effects. The occurrence and intensity of the effects of sexual assault seem, from the research, to be directly related to the closeness of the relationship between the victim and the perpetrator, the age of the victims when sexual contact began and the duration of the abuse (Wyatt & Mickey, 1987).

Myth # 5

It's really the parents' fault, because they should protect the child.

Reality

Parents are often accused of 'not protecting the child' in cases of sexual assault, whether or not they know about it. This attitude shifts the blame and allows the real offenders to avoid responsibility for their actions.

Myth # 6

A reason some people use to excuse child sexual offenders is to argue that as a child the offender was abused and therefore it's not their fault because they can't help it.

Reality

As discussed early in the section on offenders, Finkelhor's (1984) preconditions for sexual offending recognises that the motivation to offend may include emotional congruence, which can result from being sexually assaulted as a child. In addition, the absence of internal inhibitions to sexually offend against a child may be related to childhood experiences. However, research has shown that most people who have been sexually assaulted do not go on to sexually assault their own or other people's children (Briggs, 1995).

Myth # 7

Men who sexually assault boys are homosexual.

Reality

Most men who molest boys are heterosexual (Smallbone & Wortley, 2000). There is no evidence that homosexual men sexually assault boys any more than heterosexual men.

Myth # 8

Incest and sexual assault only occurs in poor families.

Reality

Incest and sexual assault may occur in families rich or poor, large or small, well educated or not.

Myth # 9

The child never said no, or tried to stop the sexual assault, so it's the child's fault if they're assaulted.

Reality

For many reasons children may not be able to say 'no'. It's always the offenders who are responsible, whatever happened.

Myth # 10

Children and young people lie or fantasise about sexual assault.

Reality

Some adults prefer to believe this. Research has shown that in 98% of reports by children, their statements were found to be true (Dympna House, 1998).

It is extremely unlikely that minors will lie about sexual assault. The reality is that it takes a great deal of courage for victims of child sexual assault to come forward. When they do share their secret with someone, they should be believed. If the sexual assault did not occur, discrepancies in the repeated story will begin to surface. A made-up disclosure of sexual assault, though rare, cannot be ignored. It is an indication of some issue in the child or young person's life. Counselling is an absolute necessity in such cases.

Myth # 11

Incest or child sex is quite acceptable in some cultures.

Reality

There is no evidence to support this idea, although the cultural significance of incest and child sex and the meaning of 'child' and 'childhood' may vary in different cultures and has certainly altered over time.

Myth # 12

It's not the sexual assault that is harmful; it's all the fuss that the adults, child protection authorities and legal systems make that is the problem.

Reality

In some cases intervention by legal, medical and welfare personnel can be distressing. This shouldn't be used as an excuse by people to not speak out and to allow sexual assault to continue. Most children describe negative effects during the time they were sexual assaulted.

Prevalence statistics

Forty-five per cent of females and 19% of males have been the victim of 'non-contact inclusive' child sexual abuse and 39% of females and 13% of males have been the victim of 'non-contact exclusive' child sexual abuse (Goldman & Padayachi, 1997).

It is estimated that one in four girls and between one in seven and one in twelve boys are victims of sexual abuse (James, 2000).

Girls and boys of all ages are sexually abused and victims are sometimes toddlers, young children and even babies (NSW Child Protection Council, 2000).

In spite of the high non-disclosure rates and the difficulty in substantiating abuse, during 2000–2001 a total of 3,794 cases of sexual abuse against children in Australia were substantiated (Australian Institute of Health and Welfare, 2002).

Thirteen per cent of calls to the New South Wales Rape Crisis Centre were related to child sexual assault (*Sun Herald*, 8th January 2006. p. 7).

Research shows a staggering 45% of women aged 18–41 were sexually abused as children by family members (30%), friends or family friends (50%) or strangers (14%). 75% of the abuse involved some contact, most of which was shockingly severe (Watson, 2007).

A University of Queensland study found that 10.5% of males and 20.6% of females reported non-penetrative child sexual assault before the age of 16, and 7.5% of males and 7.9% of females reported penetrative child sexual assault before the age of 16 (Mamun et al., 2007).

Australian Bureau of Statistics report that 25% of victims of 'all' sexual assaults reported are aged between 10 and 14 (Australian Bureau of Statistics, 2009).

Disclosure and reporting statistics

In 98% of all child abuse cases reported to officials, children's statements were found to be true (Dympna House, 1998).

A 1998 study involving 400 clients of Family Planning Qld found 55% of all the women in the sample had experienced childhood sexual assault before the age of 16. Only 36% of those who had experienced assault had ever told anyone of those events prior to their disclosure during the study interview. Only eight victims (3.5%) had taken legal action against their offenders and only five were aware of the outcome of those actions (two offenders were convicted, two had no further action taken and one resulted in a criminal record only; Queensland Criminal Justice Commission, 1999).

About half of the victims of child sexual assault never report the assault to another person and many do not disclose until they reach adulthood (Queensland Crime Commission, 2000).

Project Axis sought information from 66 non-government schools about their policies for dealing with suspected child sexual assault — only six had a specific policy in place. Of the 51 community groups contacted only three had established any policy for handling suspicions or disclosures of child sexual assault (Queensland Crime Commission, 2000).

One hundred and sixty-nine child sex offenders who admitted having committed at least one sexual offence against a child later disclosed offences concerning 1,010 children (748 boys and 262 girls) of which only 393 (38.9%) were reported to have been associated with official convictions (Smallbone & Wortley, 2000).

One in five parents who were aware that their child had been sexually assaulted did not report the assault (Smallbone & Wortley, 2000).

One in three people in NSW suspect a child they know has been sexually assaulted but 43% of those did not report the abuse to authorities (Department of Community Services, 2006).

One third of people surveyed felt they only had a minor role to play in protecting children (Department of Community Services, 2006).

Seventy-eight per cent of people surveyed had some hesitation about whether they would be able to identify abuse of neglect if they came across it (Department of Community Services, 2006).

Offender statistics

The age profile of offenders in sexual assault varies with the nature of the crime. In the US in 2000 it was reported that overall, 23% of sexual assault offenders were under age 18 and 77% were adults. Juveniles were a substantially smaller proportion of the offenders in forcible rape (17%) than in sexual assaults with an object (23%), forcible fondling (27%) and incidents of forced sodomy (36%) (Bureau of Justice Statistics, 2000).

In the US, 2,000 Catholic priests have been disgraced because of their abusive behaviour, with many facing prosecution in the criminal courts (*Hansard*, 2002).

International research suggests that sex offenders are generally older than most other types of offenders. The mean age of over 9,000 sex offenders was found to be 36 years (Hanson et al., 2002).

Most children know the perpetrator, with studies estimating between 10–30% of offenders were strangers (National Child Protection Clearinghouse, 2005).

Non-biological family members (stepfather or mother's defacto) are disproportionately represented as child sex offenders. For example, Russell (1989) reported that girls living with stepfathers were at a markedly increased risk: 17% had been sexually assaulted compared with 2.3% of girls living with biological fathers (National Child Protection Clearinghouse, 2005).

Female sex offenders are responsible for 6% of all reported cases of sexual assault against children (ChildWise study, cited in *The Australian*, 7 March 2006)

Men were by far the greatest perpetrators of sexual assault, responsible for 663 cases compared to only 63 (8.7%) by women (Department of Child Safety, 2007).

For the offence of sexual assault, 34% of defendants were aged 45 and over (Australian Bureau of Statistics, 2007).

Statistics on convicting, treating and managing sex offenders

According to Weatherburn (2001) in Australia:

- Only 1 in 100 (1%) sex offenders in a given year ends up convicted of sexual assault.
- Each year in NSW, about 40,000 women will be sexually assaulted.
- About 1.000 men will be brought to court for sexual assault and about 400 of those men will either plead guilty or be found guilty.

Only about 17% of reported sexual offences result in a conviction, a figure consistent with data from other States and overseas (Queensland Crime and Misconduct Commission, 2003).

Results from 69 different studies found that treated sex offenders reoffended sexually 37% less than untreated offenders (Losel & Schmucker, 2005).

Less than 2% of cases reported to police, where the offender is a female, result in a jail term, compared with 16.5% of cases involving men (ChildWise study, cited in *The Australian*, 7 March 2006).

Ninety per cent of reported sex assaults do not end up in convictions and only 17% of reported sex assaults proceed to court (Fitzgerald, 2006).

Hoy and Bright (2008) reported that 8.5% of sex offenders who were treated at the CUBIT programs committed a further sexual offence in the follow-up period (3.75 years) compared with the predicted sexual recidivism rate of 26%.

Chapter 1: Review questions

1. Review the examples of sexual assault on pages 11–12. Which do you think are examples of situational offenders and which are examples of preferential offenders? What factors have you taken into consideration?
2. Think of an example for each of the grooming techniques discussed.
3. List some of the effects of child sexual assault that may be specific to children offended against by a family member. Why might intrafamilial sexual assault impact on victims differently to extrafamilial offences?
4. Identify a myth about child sexual assault that you thought was true. How do you feel about that myth now?
5. Consider five statistics on child sexual assault that surprise you. What is it about these statistics that you find astounding?

Chapter 2

Dealing with Disclosures

The aim of this chapter is to provide practitioners with information about the legal aspects associated with responding to, documenting and reporting disclosures. Practitioners are often unsure about how to respond appropriately to a disclosure of sexual assault as they do not want to re-traumatise their client or impede any potential legal outcome. It is important that professionals feel comfortable in their ability to respond appropriately to disclosures of sexual assault, as well as advise parents on how best to support their child following sexual assault, as an appropriate response can be a positive turning point in the client's healing process.

Chapter overview

1. Information regarding mandatory reporting requirements in Australia.
2. Effective therapeutic responses to disclosures in session.
3. Information about making a report.
4. Supporting parents to respond effectively to disclosures and understand the emotions their child may be experiencing.
5. Supporting parents who have their own sexual assault history and understanding how this may impact on how they respond to their child's experience.
6. Documentation and case notes.

Upon completion of this chapter it is intended that you:

1. have an understanding of your responsibilities with regard to mandatory reporting requirements
2. feel an increased sense of confidence when responding to a client's disclosure of sexual assault
3. have an enhanced ability to support and advise parents appropriately
4. will maintain appropriate case notes and documentation.

Mandatory reporting

The introduction of mandatory reporting requires that certain professionals report cases of child sexual assault or child abuse cases to their state or territory's child protection authorities when they have reasonable grounds to suspect a child has been, or is being, harmed. The concept of 'reasonable grounds' can be difficult to comprehend. Generally, reasonable grounds are a belief that a child may be in need of protection based on situations where:

- a child states that they have been sexually assaulted or abused
- a child states that they know someone who has been sexually assaulted or abused (sometimes the child may be talking about themselves)
- a relative, friend, acquaintance or sibling of the child states that the child has been sexually assaulted or abused
- professional observations of the child's behaviour or development lead the mandated professional to form a belief that the child has been sexually assaulted or abused; and /or
- signs of sexual assault or abuse lead to a belief the child may have been abused.

Remember that it is not your role to investigate these concerns; this is the role of child protection authorities and the police.

Mandatory reporting legislation clarifies the actions of professionals who suspect a child is being harmed and removes any concerns in regard to confidentiality issues. Some advantages of mandatory reporting are to:

- increase protection of children
- clarify community and government expectations about reporting
- reduce discretion of professionals as to whether or not they should report
- minimise harmful effects of child sexual assault and child abuse when intervention takes place as soon as possible.

It is important for everyone working in this sector, or working with children and young people (including parents and children), to understand the legislative and mandatory reporting obligations for both disclosure and concerns around child protection issues.

The best way to be prepared and protect against any concerns is to ensure that your service or organisation has documented policy and procedures that include information on:

- what should be reported
- when to report
- who to report to
- how to report (verbal, documentation, standardised forms)
- processes that will follow the report.

Each state and territory and each sector has differing legislative requirements in respect to child protection and reporting policies. These requirements regularly change. It is important that all individuals and organisations whose work involves children or brings them into regular contact with children are aware of their obligations. This should be articulated in your documented policy and procedures. If you or your organisation comes under this legislation, penalties apply if you fail to report concerns.

Regardless of whether or not your industry is subject to mandatory reporting, anyone who has reasonable grounds should report known or suspected harm to a child or young person.

Responding to a disclosure in session

Your response to any disclosure of child sexual assault can be the first step in protecting the child from further harm and the first step to guarantee the child's safety and wellbeing.

When a child discloses sexual assault or abuse they will more than likely be experiencing negative feelings, including fear, anxiety, guilt, shame, anger, confusion and powerlessness. It is important to provide an appropriate response, even if you are unsure about the truthfulness of the disclosure or concerns.

This initial response can vary depending on circumstances and needs. Responses may consist of implementing protective strategies, engaging appropriate services and/or making reports to relevant authorities. No matter what the initial response is, it is important that the child's wellbeing and safety be assured at each and every step.

If you suspect child sexual assault, but no disclosure has been made, always remain aware of the emotional distress the child may be experiencing. Approach the child in a caring and sensitive manner by assuring them that you are there to listen, and that you will help if there is a problem.

It is important that you do not ask any direct questions about what happened (the 'who', 'how', 'where' questions) as these may taint any future investigations. Use open ended questions that allow the child to express how they are feeling:

> *I have noticed you seem a bit sad lately. I want you to know that if I am here if you would like to tell me anything.*

If a child does disclose sexual assault or harm to you, avoid direct questions about what happened. Instead, reflect back to the child and let them know that you can help:

> *Wow, so he made you feel sad, is there anything else you would like to tell me?*
>
> *I am so sorry that happened to you. I will do everything I can to help you stay safe.*

If a disclosure has been made, use this checklist to help best support the child:

LISTEN: Listen carefully to all that they say.

AFFIRM: Tell the child that you believe them.

DON'T BLAME: Let the child know that what has happened is not their fault.

ENCOURAGE: Tell the child that they are not responsible for the assault and that you know it must have been difficult for them to tell you.

SAFETY: Let the child know that you will do everything in your power to help them.

DOCUMENT: Write everything down, using the child's own words as best you can, include behaviours and any things they have said previously that may have hinted at the assault.

CHECK: Check your organisation's policy on reporting disclosures.

ACT: To ensure the best interests of the child, report the disclosure to your state's statutory child protection authority or the police.

To be effective, child protection practices must be holistically applied in your organisation. Being able to respond effectively and appropriately are key to ensuring that you can best support the children who attend.

Making a report

Each state and territory has different legislation and guidelines around reporting child protection concerns. It is a good idea to familiarise yourself with the process so you will know how to respond if any concerns arise.

Remember:

- When you make a report, your details are kept confidential and your identity is strictly protected.
- You don't need permission from your organisation to report concerns; however, there may be procedures and policies in place that will help support you through this process.
- You should make a report each time you become aware of further grounds for your concerns.
- There is no need for you to 'prove' that harm has occurred. As long as you have reasonable grounds for reporting, it is up to the authorities to investigate.

The information you pass on to the authorities should include:

- details — the child's or young person's name, age and address
- indicators of harm — the reason for believing that there are child protection concerns
- reason for reporting — the reason why the call is being made now
- safety assessment — assessment of immediate danger to the child or children (e.g., information may be sought on the whereabouts of the alleged abuser or abusers)
- the current whereabouts of the child or young person
- your knowledge of other services involved with the family
- any other information about the family
- specific characteristics — any specific cultural or other details that will help to care for the child (e.g., interpreter needs or disability needs).

Please note — a notification should still be made even if you do not have all the information listed above.

Once you have made a report the child protection service can:

- provide further advice to you
- investigate your concerns
- ensure that the child or young person is safe.

The police will be able to:

- investigate your concerns
- pursue avenues for criminal matters
- work with the child protection service.

Assisting parents to respond effectively to disclosures

Some do's for parents after disclosure

Bravehearts' therapists have found that children who have supportive, caring, and understanding caregivers usually experience fewer ill effects than those children who do not. Parents play a very important role in a child's recovery by providing reassurance, safety and love; each child needs to know that they are supported and believed.

Below is a list of things parents may choose to say to their child after they have disclosed sexual assault:

- 'Thank you for telling me. I believe you.'
- 'I am sorry this happened to you.'
- 'You don't have to worry about taking care of me; the adults are responsible for taking care of things.'
- 'I know this was not your fault.'
- 'That must have been really hard to tell me about.'
- 'I am sad/angry/upset this happened to you. You may see me cry but that is ok. I am not sad/angry/upset at you at all and I can take care of myself.'
- 'This has happened in other families; we are not alone and we will get through this together.'
- 'I am sorry I did not realise this was happening to you. Now I know what you were trying to tell me.'

Encourage parents to let their child know that they may need to tell other people about what has happened so they can help, such as the police, counsellor or teacher; and that this is okay. It is important for the secrecy and silence to be broken down and that the child and parent/carer know that it is okay to talk about what happened. For healing to occur it is vital that the child, parent and family have safe avenues for talking about what happened and how they feel about the harm and the person who harmed them.

Remember that the experience of sexual assault often undermines children's sense of safety. Children may become more clingy, be afraid at bedtime, or need to have their parents near them more frequently, all of which are very common and normal behaviours. Children often need a lot of reassurance during this time so explain to parents not to fear they may be 'spoiling' them by giving them the security, reassurance, and attention that they need.

Some don'ts for parents after disclosure

When a child is sexually assaulted parents can often feel an array of emotions: sadness, grief, rage, disbelief, numbness, to name a few. Let them know that they have every right to feel whatever they are feeling, and allowing themselves to be sad or angry or to cry, shows their child that this behaviour is acceptable and reasonable. However, it is important that the parent explains their feelings and reactions to their child as they experience them and to reassure them that the child is not responsible for them feeling this way.

Children often believe they are the cause of everything that happens in their world and can feel they are to blame for the parent's responses and reactions too. Explain to parents that it is wise to keep explosive reactions and behaviours such as 'I want to kill the ___', 'This family has been destroyed' for other adults. Children can understand and deal with their caregivers' emotions when they are not too overwhelming or scary.

Below is a list of things that can be unhelpful to a child after disclosure, and should be discussed with the parent:

- Be careful not to put too many limits on the child's play or activities any more than needed to feel peace of mind — they may see this as a form of punishment.
- Don't make promises that cannot be kept, such as 'You never have to see him again', or that the perpetrator will get what they deserve/go to jail.
- Don't urge the child to 'forget about it'.

- Do not berate the child because they didn't tell about the abuse sooner — children have very good reasons (both real and imagined) as to why they don't tell about their abuse and this type of questioning can increase their feelings of guilt.
- Don't ask them why they didn't say 'No'. This question assumes that the child had a choice in being assaulted. They didn't.
- Don't let the child feel as though they are responsible for any pain or disruption in the family because they told about what was happening to them.
- Do not play the role of investigator and ask direct questions about the hows, whats and whys of the assault — sometimes children cannot find the words, feel embarrassed, feel it's their fault, or feel the pressure in a parent's reaction, and may decide to 'forget' the whole thing. Also, this line of questioning is not helpful in terms of any police involvement there may be now or in the future.
- Don't assume they are lying about their experiences — children do lie, most often as a way to avoid punishment or getting into trouble, but research suggests that most do not lie about sexual matters.

Is my child damaged forever?

Supporting parents in understanding their child

Popular media would have people believe that once a child has been sexually assaulted their life trajectory is clear — drug use, promiscuity, learning difficulties, prostitution, sexual offending. In reality, research and anecdotal evidence suggests that almost half of children who have experienced sexual assault show no adverse negative reactions 6–12 months after the event (Caffaro-Rouget, Lang, & Van Santen, 1989).

Although it is often believed that children who have experienced more frequent, intrusive sexual assault by a close family member in comparison experience more difficulties, this is not always the case; in fact these children may even fare better than those who experience a single traumatic episode. The key point here is that each child's experience of sexual assault is unique and must be responded to in a sensitive and caring way.

What is clear is that it is the amount and type of support a child receives after their disclosure that makes all the difference. As a therapist, spending time with parents is beneficial as it may assist them to better support their child following a traumatic event.

Parents who have their own sexual assault history

It is not uncommon for parents to also have their own sexual assault history, and this certainly adds a complicating dimension to therapy. Exploring with the parent how their own assault was handled (if at all), what benefit it was to them and what was harmful, will give you insight into their values and how they might be dealing (or not dealing) with their child's own sexual assault. Connecting parents to how they want the experience to be different for their child, and exploring their resources and motivations to do this, are also important.

It is sometimes the case that a parent or caregiver (whether or not they are a survivor of childhood abuse themselves) are extremely traumatised upon discovering that their child has been sexually assaulted. It is understandable that this would be a terrible situation to confront as a parent. However, it is not helpful for the child if the parents' own trauma response is so overwhelming that it is projected onto the child. It is sometimes the case that a parent is assuming that the feelings they are personally experiencing are mirroring those being felt by the child. However, in some cases the child may be coping quite well and it is the confusing and overwhelming response of the parent that may prove therapeutically detrimental to the child.

In this case it is helpful to provide the parent with an opportunity to vent and explore their feelings without the child present. It is often recommended that personal counselling is organised for the parent or caregiver to help them come to terms with what has occurred and therefore assist them to be more emotionally available to best support their child's needs. One of the most therapeutic aspects for the child can be having a parent who is emotionally present, calm, loving and reassuring, not caught up with their own anger, grief, confusion and sadness.

Supporting parents so that they are able to support their children is an important part of the counselling process. It can also play an important role in changing any dysfunctional intergenerational behaviours that impede communication and healing within a family.

Documentation and case notes

Counsellors should write case notes regarding each session they have with a client as soon as possible after the session. Usually the notes are a recording of the activities undertaken during the session. Notes can include any caregiver feedback, the child's presentation during the session, and the general content of the session or therapeutic interventions undertaken. It is important in case notes that a therapist does not include their interpretation of children's play or conversation, but to simply document what they have observed in the counselling room.

If at any point a child discloses sexual assault, it is recommended that the conversation is recorded verbatim in the case notes, where possible. It is also advised that the case notes contain information regarding what was happening in the lead up to the disclosure as well as the therapist's response to the disclosure.

If a child does make a disclosure, it is recommended that the therapist attend to the child's feelings about what happened. It is not recommended that the therapist ask any further direct questions to obtain additional information from the child. It is often the case that simply attending to the child's feelings around their disclosure is enough to elicit further self-disclosure. The main rule to remember is that, in every instance your role as a practitioner is therapeutic, not investigatory.

Example of a poor therapeutic response

Client: 'My grandpa touched my penis and I didn't like it.'

Therapist: 'Did he? What else has he done to you?'

Client: 'I don't know.'

Therapist: 'Well, has he touched you anywhere else?'

Client: 'No … I don't want to talk anymore …'

Example of an appropriate therapeutic response

Client: 'My grandpa touched my penis and I didn't like it.'

Therapist: 'You didn't like it?'

Client: 'No, it felt yucky.'

Therapist: 'It sounds as though you were having a "no" feeling when that happened?'

Client: 'Yeah, I told him to stop but he didn't.'

As these examples demonstrate the therapist can often gain more relevant information by giving the child the room and the opportunity to fully express their emotional experience of the assault rather than asking investigatory and invasive questions.

Chapter 2: Review questions

1. Do you think the mandatory reporting requirements in your state or territory are sufficient? If not, what do you think needs to be changed?

2. If you were concerned about a neighbour's child, would you report your concerns? What are some of the reasons for reporting? What are some of the reasons for not reporting?

3. If a 16-year-old client disclosed that she was engaging in promiscuous behaviour, how would you respond?

4. Review your organisation's/industry's policies with respect to disclosures.

5. What are some of the reasons that a parent may not respond appropriately to a child's disclosure to them? How would you address these?

Chapter 3

The Therapeutic Process: Common Presenting Problems

The aim of this chapter is to introduce a number of common emotional and behavioural symptoms that clients present with in counselling, and highlight some important considerations regarding the therapeutic process when working with children and young people affected by sexual assault.

Chapter overview

1. Common presenting problems associated with child sexual assault.
2. The therapeutic process.
3. Discussing the sexual assault.

Upon completion of this chapter it is intended that you:

1. will be able to identify several common presenting problems associated with child sexual assault
2. have an increased awareness of the therapeutic process in order to place the techniques from the Bravehearts' toolbox into context when used during counselling
3. have an increased understanding on whether it is ever appropriate to discuss the specific details of the sexual assault with a client.

Common presenting problems

As outlined in Chapter 1, there are a number of short- and long-term impacts of child sexual assault. At Bravehearts client presentations vary widely. However, some issues appear more commonly than others. Some of the most common presentations include:

Anger

Often children feel a strong sense of anger, which may be directed at themselves, the offender, and/or family members. Often this anger manifests in aggressive behaviour. This is most often directed at people who the child feels the least threatened by. Examples of aggressive behaviour include fighting at school or at home, throwing objects at others, punching/hitting objects, inappropriate yelling/screaming at others. This may present in the counselling room with aggressive play. It is important to acknowledge and validate the source/s of this anger, while at the same time, highlighting to the child the importance of channelling this anger in appropriate ways so as not to hurt or upset any one else in the process.

Boundaries

Due to the intrusive nature of child sexual assault, children are often confused about boundaries and personal space. They may not have a sense of appropriate personal space, and may often intrude on other people's personal space when interacting with them. This may not only be uncomfortable for those people in contact with the child, but can also place the child at further risk. This may present in the counselling room, with the child wanting to sit in your lap, sit right next to you, persistently hugging you, wanting to extend the allocated counselling time, and break rules etc.

Rapport building and trust

Often, due to the fact that someone they trusted violated them, children's levels of trust can be shattered. This can lead to difficulty making and maintaining peer friendships, shyness and withdrawal when meeting new people — especially adults — and an inability to trust some or all adults. This often makes rapport-building with clients more challenging, and it may have to be built over several sessions before the child trusts the relationship enough to open up to you. It is important that the activity you choose to introduce to the child allows for this trust, and your relationship with one another, to build.

Sleeping problems

Sleeping problems, especially nightmares, difficulty falling and staying asleep, an inability to sleep in one's own bed, and being scared of the dark are all problems associated with a child's feelings of a lack of safety following sexual assault and can become a larger problem for the family as a unit. Children will often be happy to discuss, draw/paint or use mediums such as a sand tray to act out the nightmares they have. They may be able to verbalise what scares them about bed time and these images can then be used as a therapeutic tool to reduce the anxiety associated with sleeping and bed time.

Fear

Fear can manifest in all areas of the child's life, including bed time as previously noted. Some other examples of fear include fear of being left alone for periods of time; fear of new adults entering the home; fear of the offender coming to 'get' them; and symbolic fear (e.g., monsters under the bed). Some children may become hypervigilant and exist in a constant state of 'fight or flight'. This is often related to the child feeling powerless. It is important then to instil renewed feelings of empowerment in the child.

Avoidance

Children who have experienced child sexual assault sometimes develop strategies, that become coping mechanisms to enable day-to-day functioning, whereby they detach from the emotional and physical pain of events, especially when the harm continues over a long period of time. Typical avoidance strategies employed by children include: denial, forgetting (repressing memories), dissociation and displacement.

Feelings

Helping a child to become in touch with their feelings is very important after a traumatic experience. A very gentle way for a child to communicate their feelings is through art. Invite them to draw a picture of how they are feeling when they suddenly become angry or scared or anxious. Be careful not to interpret what they have drawn, but instead ask questions, such as 'Can you tell me what is happening in your picture?' 'You have used the colour yellow a lot, what does that colour mean in your picture?' 'What does that colour feel like in your body?' Remember to thank them for sharing this with you.

Negative self-thoughts

Children who have been sexually assaulted commonly present negative thoughts and statements about themselves that become the child's pervasive internalised view of themselves and of external situations. Negative thoughts are often related to low self-esteem, guilt, embarrassment and self-blame.

Self-esteem

Low self-esteem is common among children who have been sexually assaulted. Children may experience low self-esteem as a constant feeling of worthlessness, repetitive voices telling them they are not good enough, or feelings that they do not deserve to feel happy or experience good things.

Self-blame and responsibility

Due to the personal nature of child sexual assault, and often because these experiences occur within already established relationships, the child may assume responsibility and blame themselves for the assault. Often the grooming techniques used, as well as the powerful dynamics between the adult and the child lead to feelings of guilt and shame which can have adverse affects for the child's self-image and development.

Keeping these symptoms in mind, the activities in the following chapter are designed to provide a basic foundation for you to build upon as a practitioner.

The therapeutic process

While learning different techniques is beneficial for any practising therapist, practitioners must always remain actively aware of the therapeutic process itself. It is important to be mindful of the powerful position a therapist has when engaged in counselling children and/or young people. There are inherent ethical and professional boundaries by which practitioners must abide to ensure that the counselling process does not have any adverse consequences for the child. Some of the main issues that must be considered at all stages of the therapeutic process include:

Reactions of the counsellor in the counselling room

It is important that counsellors be mindful of their reactions within the counselling room — the way we respond can either confirm or start to challenge some of the fears children feel about what they have experienced. These reactions can sometimes provoke negative reactions or inhibit children from engaging effectively in counselling and yet can facilitate healing regardless of whether the child discloses assault.

Counter-transference

This is particularly important for counsellors who have had difficult childhoods. Counsellors have to be particularly careful with this demographic of children. Over-identification with the situation and/or the child can lead to the therapist losing their objectivity by assuming that their own experience is the same as their clients.

Consistency and predictability

Due to the nature of child sexual assault, the importance of consistency and predictability in the counselling room can not be understated. It is imperative that the therapist establish and maintain appropriate boundaries in a reassuring and consistent manner throughout the entire counselling process.

The use of silence

Often what a child needs is time. Allowing space for the child to reply to questions or activities opens them up for discussion about emotions and behaviours. It is important however that silence is not overused or it may be viewed as punitive.

Normalising and validating the child's experience

Normalising and validating the child's experience may be the single most important strategy a practitioner can engage in to assist the healing process. Most child sexual assaults begin when the child is in an egocentric developmental stage. So often statements such as 'I've worked with many children and often they feel that way too' can assist to normalise for the child their emotions and behaviours and help them to process their experience and begin to heal.

Risk of suggestibility and leading clients

It is important that as a practitioner you remain aware of the inherent vulnerability of this client group due to their age, physical and emotional development. The importance of language can not be understated. The practitioner must always remain mindful of the possibility of suggestibility when opening conversations to elicit discussions about their client's experience.

When opening discussions it is important that open, non-leading questions are used rather than specific, closed questions. The fact that case notes can be subpoenaed makes this issue even more important.

Being the advocate for the child, not the parents

Throughout therapy it is vital to remember that the wellbeing of the child is always paramount. This is especially important in cases where parents are separated and one of the parents has been accused of the sexual assault (or where family court is involved). Hence, all decisions must be made with regard to the best interests of the child, regardless of who is bringing the child to counselling.

The role of responsibility and shame in child sexual assault

The level of responsibility and shame associated with child sexual assault can impede the counselling process. It is important that practitioners' approach is client-centred and gently assists the child to process the events at their own pace.

The role of attachment and the necessity of including the family in treatment

Often, what seems to make the most significant difference to a child is the quality of attachments they have in their lives. Thus, it is important to increase the child's support network and collaborate with the family in counselling. When working with the client's family you may find yourself asking: 'Why are these people responding in this way? Why can't they see this is counterproductive?' It can be difficult to work with families, especially when you feel that nothing you are suggesting is being implemented at home. It is important that these issues are broached gently with the family to ensure that the counselling process advances.

Discussing the sexual assault

Practitioners often ask 'Do we need to talk about the assault in counselling in order for healing to occur?' The answer to this important question is quite simply, 'no'. It is not necessary to discuss the sexual assault during counselling in order for healing to occur. In fact, it is very important that when practitioners address the assault or trauma in counselling, that they do so without the risk of re-traumatising the client.

If a child has made a disclosure prior to commencing counselling (e.g., the child has disclosed to a parent or carer, the police or a child protection worker) then letting the child know that you know what has happened to them in an age-appropriate and gentle manner and that you believe and support them can be very helpful. Often, it is the silence and lack of appropriate response to a child's disclosure that can cause further damage. For example, at Bravehearts, a therapist might let a child know in an initial session that 'Bravehearts is a place that kids come to when something yucky has happened to them. Mum has told me that someone might have done something yucky to you. I am someone that you can talk to about that and about how it made you feel, if you want to. This is a safe space for you to talk about anything you want to.'

Some children will then use the counselling experience to discuss and verbally explore the sexual assault with the support of their counsellor. Other children may decide to never mention or discuss the sexual assault during the counselling process; however, they may use the expressive therapies offered in counselling to explore and process the feelings associated with the assault in either a verbal or non-verbal manner.

Disclosure must remain the choice of the child. Whether the client chooses to discuss the sexual assault itself, work on the associated feelings, or deal with another issue altogether (e.g., being bullied at school, grief and loss issues) the counselling process can still be ultimately beneficial and result in a reduction of trauma symptoms for the child.

In fact, talking about the details of the assault can sometimes be detrimental to the therapeutic process. The reason for this is twofold: pushing a child to discuss the details of the assault when they do not wish to do so can be re-traumatising and it can also contaminate any legal proceedings that may occur as a result of the incident. Therefore, as therapists you must remain very mindful at all times that you operate purely from a therapeutic perspective, and never an investigative one. It is never the role of the therapist to investigate; this is the role of the authorities, such as the police or child protection officers.

So to summarise:

- It is important that if and when you address trauma that you do so without re-traumatising the child or young person.
- It is acceptable to acknowledge that the sexual assault has occurred, where disclosures have been made, but it must remain the choice of the client whether they wish to discuss this further.
- Explain at the very outset of counselling (intake and/or beginning of first session), in an age-appropriate manner, the concept of confidentiality and it's limits, so that the client understands your duty of care in relation to reporting current assault or risk of harm.
- Let the child know that you know what has happened and that you believe and support them.
- Talking about the details of the assault is not necessary in order for healing to commence and can in fact be harmful if there are legal processes in action surrounding the offences (see Chapter 2 for information regarding documentation and case notes).
- Many of the techniques used in working generally with trauma can be adapted to working with children who have been sexually assaulted. It is important to remember at all times that working holistically with the client's experience, not the sexual assault, itself is the most effective way of working therapeutically with this client group.

Chapter 3: Review questions

1. List five common presenting problems in children who have been sexually assaulted. How might each of these be linked to grooming techniques?
2. What would be an example of a positive and negative reaction in the counselling room?
3. What do you think may be the consequence of over-identification with a client?
4. What are some examples of appropriate boundaries that may be role-modelled by the therapist in the counselling room?
5. What do you think are some of the consequences of shame on the victim?

Chapter 4

The Therapeutic Process: Effective Approaches to Presenting Problems

The aim of this chapter is to introduce effective therapeutic approaches to use when working with children and young people affected by sexual assault. It includes some basic therapeutic tools developed to assist children in processing their experience and their associated thoughts and feelings. It provides a basic counselling toolbox for utilisation in your workplace setting.

Chapter overview

1. Suggested materials for the counselling room.
2. Techniques from the Counsellor's Toolbox.

Upon completion of this chapter it is intended that you:

1. will be able to apply some of these therapeutic interventions to clients presenting at your workplace, specifically addressing the common presenting problems outlined in Chapter 3
2. have an increased confidence to work effectively and therapeutically in response to common presenting problems within the counselling room.

Materials

When working with children and young people (and even adults) it is helpful to have a well-resourced counselling room, where possible. Basically, the more resources available, the better. Some of the materials you may need for the following techniques include:

- strong cardboard boxes (shoeboxes & the type that reams of paper come in)
- butcher's paper/A3 paper/A4 paper
- sticky tape and glue
- textas, pencils, crayons and paint
- clear plastic adhesive contact
- clay
- fabric/calico
- fabric paint/permanent textas
- toy stuffing
- rice
- small plastic bags
- needle, thread and scissors
- coloured paper/gift wrap
- a variety of craft decorations (e.g., stickers, small foam shapes & letters, glitter, feathers, pipe cleaners)
- magazines
- flexible wire
- thick coloured ribbon
- thin ribbon or thick thread
- feathers and beads
- coloured cardboard
- scissors
- band-aids

Techniques

The following pages include a number of techniques that may be useful in alleviating some of the more common effects of child sexual assault, such as anger and sleeping issues. However, it is important to realise that the client is a whole person, not a list of trauma symptoms to be methodically worked through with a variety of 'techniques'. The most important factors for healing with this client group, is that they feel believed, supported and safe from further harm. Therefore, the most important skills that the therapist can possess are genuine empathy and compassion, and the ability to build rapport with their client and meet them where they are at, at all times. These are skills that most therapists naturally possess and it is important to appreciate the value of these inherent traits.

It is also very beneficial to normalise for the client any emotions and thoughts they may be having. In fact, some of the trauma symptoms they are experiencing (e.g., anger) are valid coping mechanisms that have helped the young person 'survive', whether physically, emotionally and/or psychologically. However, the counselling process is an opportunity to gently educate the child that although it is normal to experience a range of feelings such as anger, sadness, anxiety and fear, there are ways of expressing those feelings that are less destructive and more socially acceptable. This can in turn make the child's ability to function at home, school and in other environments, much easier, both for themselves and the people around them.

So while some of the techniques used by Bravehearts' therapists to encourage emotional expression are outlined here, therapists may already possess effective methods for facilitating the expression of strong emotions. While this section may add to a therapist's existing toolbox, it is important to focus on the skills you already possess, particularly the ability to create a safe, compassionate space for your client.

1. Working with anger

Children often feel a strong sense of anger, which may be directed at themselves, the offender, family members and/or peers. Often this anger manifests in aggressive behaviour. This is most often directed at people that the child feels the least threatened by. Examples of aggressive behaviour include fighting at school or at home, throwing objects at others, punching/hitting objects, inappropriate yelling/ screaming at others. This may present in the counselling room with aggressive play. It is important to acknowledge and validate the source/s of this anger, while at the same time highlighting to the child the importance of channelling this anger in appropriate ways so as not to hurt or upset any one else in the process.

Following are five activities you may consider using when counselling a client who is expressing anger or aggression in inappropriate ways. The techniques include:

1. Angry Box
2. Angry Cushion
3. Anger Release
4. Angry Pictures
5. Clay Models.

The aim of these techniques is to assist the client to examine, externalise and eventually reduce feelings and expressions of anger.

Anger Activity 1: Angry Box

Age group: 5–10 years

Materials

- cardboard box
- butcher's paper
- textas
- clear plastic contact

Instructions: Explanation to child

1. 'Sometimes when something bad has happened to someone they can be left feeling very angry. Sometimes children do not know what to do with this anger so they might end up being mean to people that they like or they may hurt people.'
2. Find out from the child if they feel their anger more in their feet or their fists, would they feel more like kicking something or punching something when they are angry? (If they would feel more like punching do the angry cushion activity).
3. Explain that we are going to make an angry box to help get the anger out in a way that does not hurt themselves or other people, or damage property. For a few minutes every day they can take their box into the garage or outside and kick it very hard to help get the angry feelings out.

Directions

1. Get a strong cardboard box (the type that reams of paper come in are ideal).
2. Cover the box in butcher's paper.
3. Using textas, allow the child to draw and write on the box about the things that make them angry. They can also write angry words and draw angry faces.
4. When the child is finished cover the box with plastic contact so that it is strong and waterproof.
5. Explain to the child that when they are kicking the box they can think about anyone or anything that has made them angry.

Information for parent/carer

Explain to the parent that this activity is designed to allow children to release their anger in a way that does not hurt themselves or anyone else. Let them know how the angry box should work and encourage them to support their child in using the box.

Notes

You may like to draw up a chart to remind the child to kick their box for a few minutes every morning and evening.

Anger Activity 2: Angry Cushion

Age group: 5–10 years

Materials

- calico fabric
- scissors
- needle and thread
- textas or fabric paint
- toy stuffing

Instructions: Explanation to child

1. 'Sometimes when something bad has happened to someone they can be left feeling very angry. Sometimes children do not know what to do with this anger so they might end up being mean to people that they like or they may hurt people.'
2. Find out from the child if they feel their anger more in their feet or their fists, would they feel more like kicking something or punching something when they are angry? (If they would feel more like kicking do the angry box activity.)
3. Explain that to help get the anger out in a way that is okay we are going to make an angry cushion. For a few minutes every day they can hit and punch their cushion very hard to help get the angry feelings out.

Directions

1. Sew a cushion from calico approximately 30 cm by 30 cm.
2. Using permanent textas or fabric paint allows the child to decorate the outside of the cushion with whatever words or drawings they choose. They might want to draw a picture on it of the person that hurt them.
3. Stuff the cushion with toy stuffing. A bag with rice in can be put in the middle to give the cushion more weight and resistance to hit.
4. Sew the cushion up.
5. Explain to the child that when they are hitting and punching their angry cushion they can think about anyone or anything that has made them angry.

Information for parent/carer

Explain to the parent that this activity is designed to allow children to release their anger in a way that does not hurt themselves or anyone else. Let them know how the angry cushion should work and encourage them to support their child in using the cushion.

Notes

You may like to draw up a chart to remind the child to hit and punch their cushion for a few minutes every morning and evening.

Anger Activity 3: Anger Release

Age group: 5–10 years

Materials

- paper
- pen

Instructions: Explanation to child

1. 'Sometimes when something bad has happened to someone they can be left feeling very angry. Sometimes children do not know what to do with this anger so they might end up being mean to people that they like or they may hurt people.'
2. Explain that anger is an energy and in the same way that happiness makes us jump around with joy, anger makes us energised but in a negative way.
3. Explain that we are going to think about other ways of letting the anger out that are not harmful to anyone.

Directions

1. With the child, write a list of the things they can do when they are feeling angry.
2. The list may include things like screaming very loudly, jumping on the bed or trampoline, listening or singing along to music turned up very loud and other ideas the child may have.
3. Explain that when they are angry and for at least 2 minutes each day they must choose an activity to do to let the anger out.

Information for parent/carer

Let the parent or carer know that you and their child have spoken about ways of releasing angry energy and that is important that the child be permitted to use some of the techniques that are on their list. If necessary engage with the parent and child to ensure that the techniques are suitable.

Anger Activity 4: Angry Pictures

Age group: 5–13 years

Materials

- large piece of paper
- textas, pencils, crayons or paint

Instructions: Explanation to child

1. 'Sometimes when something bad has happened to someone they can be left feeling very angry. Sometimes children do not know what to do with this anger so they might end up being mean to people that they like or they may hurt people.'
2. Explain that to help get the angry feelings out some children like to draw pictures of the person they are angry at and rip them up and throw them away.

Directions

1. Give the child a large piece of paper and allow them to draw or paint the person they are angry at.
2. Ask the child if there are any things that they would like to write on the picture, angry words or things they would like to say to the person if they could.
3. Ask the child what they think should happen to the picture now.
4. Allow the child to stomp on, cut up, rip or scrunch the picture.
5. Ask the child where the picture should go now.
6. The picture may be thrown away, buried or (if small enough) flushed.

Notes

Older clients may choose to burn the picture with adult assistance.

Anger Activity 5: Clay Models

Age group: 5–13 years

Materials

- clay

Instructions: Explanation to child

1. 'Sometimes when something bad has happened to someone they can be left feeling very angry. Sometimes children do not know what to do with this anger so they might end up being mean to people that they like or they may hurt people.'
2. Explain that to help get the angry feelings out some children like to make a clay model of the person they are angry at and squish them and throw them away.

Directions

1. Give the child an amount of clay.
2. Let them make a model of the person they are angry at, they may ask you to help them.
3. Allow the child to then hit, chop, squish etc the model until they are finished.
4. Ask the child what they would like to do with the clay now. They may like to throw it in the bin or lock it up in a box so that they can shake it around later if they still feel angry. Some children like to paint or write on the box.

2. Working with boundaries

Due to the intrusive nature of child sexual assault, children are often confused about boundaries and personal space. They may not have a sense of appropriate personal space and may sometimes intrude on other people's personal space when interacting with them. This may not only be uncomfortable for those people in contact with the child, but can also place the child at further risk. This may present in the counselling room, with the child wanting to sit in your lap, sit right next to you, persistently hugging you, wanting to extend the allocated counselling time, and break rules etc.

Here is an activity you may consider utilising when counselling a client who is demonstrating difficulty in maintaining inappropriate boundaries.

1. The Magic Bubble

The aim of the following technique is to provide the child with knowledge of, and the ability to, implement safe, personal boundaries.

Boundaries Activity 1: The Magic Bubble

Age group: 5–10 years

Materials

- cardboard and paper
- textas, pencils, crayons or paint

Instructions: Explanation to child

1. Explain to the child that we are going to complete an activity to learn about personal space.
2. As this is an activity that will be taken home, explain to the parent/carer the purpose of the activity

Directions

1. Introduce the activity to the child and check their understanding of what 'personal space' means.
2. Demonstrate the importance of personal boundaries with the child by asking them to stand at one end of the room, with you at the other. Each of you is to take a step closer to one another until one of you wants to take a step backwards.
3. When this point is reached, explain to the child that this is their invisible magic bubble and that people must respect this personal space, just as they too should respect others' personal space.
4. To consolidate this activity, ask the child to draw or paint their magic bubble on a sheet of cardboard or paper and have them take it home with them.

3. Rapport building and trust

Often, due to the fact that someone they trusted violated them, children's levels of trust can be shattered. This can manifest in difficulty making and maintaining peer friendships, shyness and withdrawal when meeting new people (especially adults) and an inability to trust some or all adults. This often makes rapport building with clients more challenging and it may have to be built over several sessions before the child trusts the relationship enough to open up to you. It is important that the activity you choose to introduce to the child allows for this trust, and your relationship with one another, to build.

Here is an activity that you may consider utilising when you are finding it difficult to build rapport and trust with a client:

1. The Special Box.

The aim of the following technique is to build rapport with the client and allow time to build trust in the counselling process.

Rapport Building Activity 1: The Special Box

Age group: 6–14+ years

Materials

- shoe box
- coloured paper / gift wrapping paper
- textas
- miscellaneous craft items (e.g., glitter, feathers, stickers)

Instructions: Explanation to child

1. Explain to the child we are going to make a special box that will be private for them.
2. The idea of the special box is that if you have any bad thoughts or bad dreams or feelings you can write them down or draw a picture about them and put them in your box so that you do not have to think about them so much.
3. You can show people what is in your box but no one is allowed to look in the box without your permission.

Directions

1. Introduce the shoe box to the child.
2. Cover the shoebox in paper/gift wrap of the child's choice.
3. While you cover the bottom of the box get the child to begin choosing craft items they would like to use to decorate their box.
4. Help the child (if necessary) to decorate the box and put their name on it if they wish.
5. Talk with the child about the kind of things they put in their box. Explain that they can bring their box to counselling each time if they want to show you what they have been thinking and feeling.

Information for parent/carer

As this box will be taken home, explain to the parent the purpose of the activity and the importance of ensuring the child's privacy.

4. Working with Sleeping Problems

Sleeping issues — such as nightmares, difficulty falling asleep, difficulty staying asleep, an inability to sleep in one's own bed and being scared of the dark — are problems commonly associated with sexual assault and can become a larger problem for the family as a unit.

Children and young people who have experienced sexual assault and/or other forms of trauma can often experience fear and anxiety. This is often connected to feeling unsafe and a sense of powerlessness. Any rituals or strategies that assist a child to feel safe enough to go sleep (and stay asleep) can be beneficial as being asleep is when children can feel most vulnerable. These may include leaving a night-light on, having a lock on the window, hugging a soft toy, having a pre-bedtime story, or reassuring chat with a parent/carer, even for older children and adolescents. Sometimes parents or carers are concerned that their child has 'regressed' in their sleeping habits and want to take a punitive or reward based response. Educating parents that when a child has experienced trauma or feels unsafe it is okay (in fact, it is therapeutic and beneficial) to use strategies such as nightlights to assist a child to feel safe and reassured, no matter what age their child is.

Painting nightmares or re-enacting them in sandtray and exploring alternative, positive endings can also empower a child and help lessen the incidence of sleeping issues. Anything that helps a child to feel more in control, safe and possessing some mastery over a fear-inducing person may have a beneficial effect.

Here is an activity that you may consider utilising when counselling a client who is experiencing sleeping problems:

1. Dream Catcher

The aim of the following technique is to reduce the frequency of bad dreams and increase the child's feelings of safety.

Sleeping Problems Activity 1: Dream Catcher

Age group: 6–14+ years

Materials

- flexible wire
- tape
- colourful ribbon or cord
- glue
- feathers
- beads

Instructions: Explanation to child

1. Talk about the fact that lots of children have bad dreams and sometimes a beautiful dream catcher can help to reduce the bad dreams and help them to have nice dreams.
2. As you make the dream catcher together, explain how the American Indians believe dream catchers work. (See note at end of activity.)

Directions

1. Create a ring by using flexible wire, and tape ends together.

2 Wrap the wire with coloured ribbon until the wire is completed covered and tie off, leaving enough ribbon remaining to hang the dream catcher.

3. Using thick thread (or a thin ribbon); wrap the thread around the circle to create three points around the dream catcher.

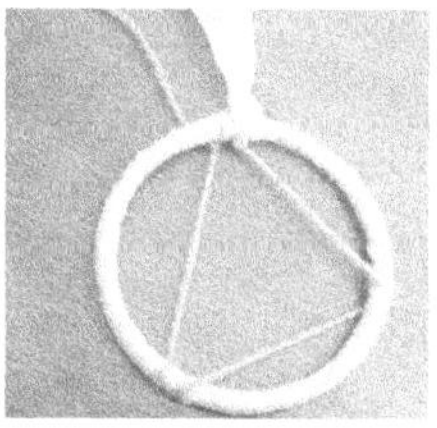

4. Using the same threading technique, being careful to keep the tension tight on the thread, continue to work towards the middle of the dream catcher to create a web.

5. Thread a bead through the ribbon and tie of to complete the 'web' End the web by putting a couple regular sewing knots on strand, cutting off the extra

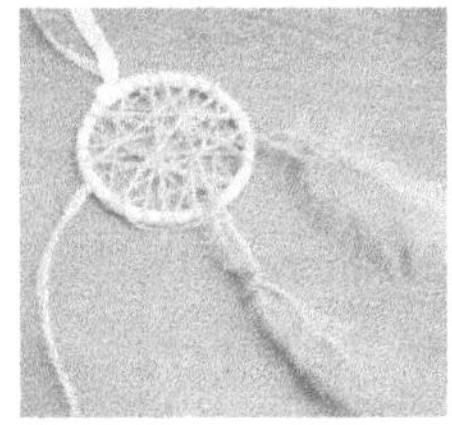

6. Cut three lengths of ribbon to tie at three points along the bottom of the dream catcher. At the bottom of each ribbon, attach three feathers threaded through a bead to complete the dream catcher

Alternatives for other age groups

- Younger children may prefer to wrap pipe cleaners around the wire instead of ribbon.
- Also, a small paper plate can be used instead of wire: cut a large hold out of the middle, so you are left with a paper ring. Punch holes at even intervals around the cardboard circle and use coloured wool to weave a 'web' between the holes.
- You can purchase metal rings or hoops from craft supply stores as a starting point, rather than making a hoop from flexible wire.

Information for parent/carer

As the dream catcher will be taken home, explain to the parent that the dream catcher needs to hang above the child's bed so that when they sleep they will feel comforted by the thought that their bad dream will be caught and stopped from bothering them.

Notes

Dream catchers originated from Native American culture and are believed to help young children by trapping bad dreams or nightmares in their web while allowing good dreams to slide down to the sleeper.

5. Working with fear

Fear can manifest in all areas of the child's life, including bed time as previously noted. Some other examples of fear include fear of being left alone for periods of time; fear of new adults entering the home; fear of the offender coming to 'get' them; and symbolic fear (e.g., monsters under the bed). Children who have experienced trauma such as sexual assault may become hypervigilant and exist in a constant state of 'fight or flight', which can easily be triggered resulting in aggressive outbursts. This is often related to the child feeling powerless. It is important then, to instil renewed feelings of empowerment in the child.

Here are seven activities you may consider utilising when counselling a client who is exhibiting or experiencing fear. The techniques are as follows:

1. Protective Shield
2. Protective Dog or Monster Picture
3. Fairy Wand and Crown
4. Magic Carpet
5. Protective Toy or Cushion
6. Superhero Self
7. Relaxation Technique.

The aim of the following techniques is to examine and reduce fear responses and increase the child's feelings of safety and personal power.

Fear Activity 1: Protective Shield

Age group: 5–10 years

Materials

- cardboard
- scissors
- pens, textas or paint
- tape

Instructions: Explanation to child

1. Talk about the things that make the child feel better when they are scared.
2. Suggest that they draw these things onto a shield to help protect them from the bad thought and feelings.
3. As this shield will be taken home, explain the purpose of the protective shield to the parent.

Directions

1. On the piece of cardboard, draw on a shield shape
2. Help the child to cut the shield out.
3. Help child (if necessary) to draw, write or otherwise represent on the shield the things that make them feel safe and happy.
4. Secure pieces of card to the back so the child can hold the shield on their arm.

Fear Activity 2: Protective Dog or Monster Picture

Age group: 5–10 years

Materials

- paper
- pens, textas or paint

Instructions: Explanation to child

1. Suggest that if they can paint a very scary dog or monster to put on the wall (or by the window or door) it will help to scare away the bad people or feelings.

Directions

1. Get a large piece of paper (stick pieces of paper together if necessary).
2. Help the child to draw monster or dog or any other scary thing they think of.
3. Help the child (if necessary) to paint picture.
4. Child can opt to write phrases such as 'stay out', 'go away' on picture.

Fear Activity 3: Fairy Wand and Crown

Age group: 5–10 years

Materials

- coloured or white cardboard
- pens or textas
- craft material such as glitter, sequins, stickers and ribbons
- 30 cm length of dowel
- glue

Instructions: Explanation to child

1. Talk to the child about their ideas about fairies and their powers.
2. Explore what wishes they would grant if they were a fairy and what wishes they would want granted for themselves.
3. Talk about how they might be able to cast spells to make the bad feelings and thoughts go away.

Directions

1. The crown can be made from coloured card or white card and painted. Help the child to draw on and cut out the points of the crown. Measure it to the size of the child's head and staple or stick in place.
2. Decorate with sequins, stickers, ribbons and so on.
3. To make the wand cut two star shapes from cardboard.
4. Cut a length of dowel and glue the stars together securing the dowel in between them.
5. Decorate the stars with glitter and sequins. Curling ribbons can also be added to the star.

Fear Activity 4: Magic Carpet

Age group: 5–10 years

Materials

- piece of carpet or doormat
- textas or permanent markers
- craft material such as glitter, sequins and ribbons
- glue

Instructions: Explanation to child

1. Talk to the child about the idea of a 'safe place'.
2. Explore with them what it would be like there and who they would invite.
3. Do the safe place visualisation activity.
4. Now suggest that to get to their safe place they could fly on a magic carpet.

Directions

1. Buy a piece of carpet or cheap doormat.
2. Help child (if necessary) to decorate the mat with curling ribbon tassels, glitter, permanent markers and any other things they choose.
3. Safe place visualisation activity
   - Ask the client to imagine a safe place.
   - Relax the client. Ask them to close their eyes and imagine that they are in this safe place.
   - Ask the client to think about all aspect of that place, how it looks, feels, what it's energy is like.
   - Now become that place.
   - Feel your body changing, change your posture if that helps.
   - Feel the energy of this place in your body.
   - Take some full breaths and feel how it is to be this place.
   - Tell me what you look like.
   - Tell me what you are made of.
   - What are your main qualities and feelings?
   - Tell me about your age. Are you old or young?
   - Do you have a sound or movement? If yes ask to demonstrate; for example if they imagine they are a willow tree, do they sway in the breeze?
   - Do you have a special purpose? What are you there for?
   - Is there anything you want?
   - Does the place have a message for (the client) or anything it wants to say to him/her? Any advice perhaps?
   - Now come back to yourself and then gently open your eyes.
   - Did you hear that message the place had for you? How does that feel?
   - After some discussion of insights and feelings ask the client to either draw the place or create a picture about the message they were given.

Fear Activity 5: Protective Toy or Cushion

Age group: 5–13 years

Materials

- piece of soft fabric
- pen
- scissors
- needle and thread
- toy stuffing
- PVA glue
- craft materials such as beads, sequins
- permanent marker

Instructions: Explanation to child

1. Explain that sewing a nice toy or cushion might make them feel safer and happier at times when they feel scared.

Directions

1. Let the child decide what shape toy or cushion they would like. Explain to them that easier shapes are easier to sew (see examples below).
2. Draw the design on a piece of paper if necessary.
3. Draw the design on the fabric and cut out the design for the child.
4. Pin the pieces together (wrong sides out) and help child to thread the needle. Sew pieces leaving an opening to stuff toy/cushion. Gauge level of help to child's age.
5. Once sewn, turn cushion/toy inside out, stuff and sew up opening. Other designs can be cut from felt and stuck on with PVA glue. Beads can also be added to decorate or drawings added using permanent markers.

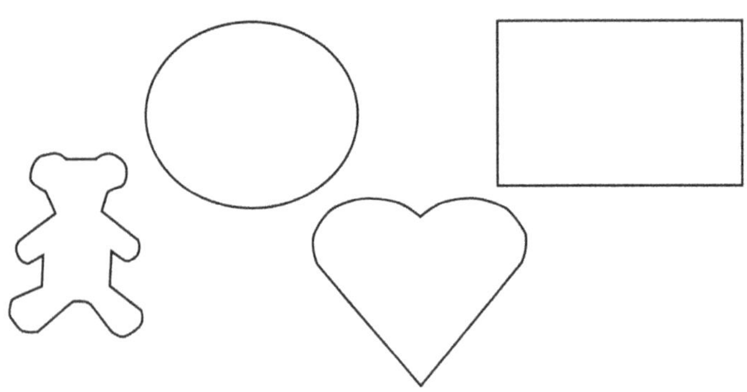

Fear Activity 6: Superhero Self

Age group: 5–13 years

Materials

- butcher's paper
- textas, paint
- craft material such as glitter, sequins, stickers and ribbons

Instructions: Explanation to child

1. Talk to the child about their favourite superhero.
2. Explore with them what powers they would want if they were a superhero.
3. Suggest to them that you help them to draw or paint their 'Superhero Self'.

Directions

1. Connect sheets of butcher's paper to make a sheet large enough for the child to lie down on.
2. If the child is comfortable with the idea ask the child to lie on the paper and draw around them (be careful not to draw close to the child's private areas; these areas of the outline can be drawn freehand later). Otherwise sketch them as life size as possible.
3. Let the child draw in their features and design their superhero costume. Paint picture and decorate.
4. Around the outside write about their super powers.

Notes

As an alternative, help the child design and make a superhero costume, including a headband, wrist bands and a shield or power stick.

Fear Activity 7: Relaxation Technique

Age group: 11–14+ years

Instructions: Explanation to child

1. Explain to the young person that with practise we can learn to control the fear responses of our body.

Directions

1. Give the young person the relaxation techniques instructions.
2. Explain that it is not important to be good at all the techniques but to be very good at one of them.
3. Explain that the more they practise the better they will become and the easier they will find it to relax themselves.

Relaxation Technique 1

- Sit or lie comfortably. Put a coin or small object in your right hand. Close your eyes and raise your right arm with the object clenched in your hand. Count one on each outward breath and on each count slowly unclench your fist. By the count of 10 the object should have dropped from your hand and your arm should be in a resting position.
- Count 1 on each outward breath. After five breaths close your eyes. Now count backwards from 50 counting each outward breath. If your thoughts wander and you lose count go back to the last number you remember counting and continue.

Relaxation Technique 2

- Sit or lie comfortably. Close your eyes. Imagine your body is hollow and a warm, white light is pouring into you starting from your toes. Feel the warmth moving up your legs relaxing your ankles then your calf muscles, your knees and so on, all the way up to your neck and face.

Relaxation Technique 3

- Lie down and close your eyes. Progressively move your concentration up your body tensing and relaxing each muscle in turn.

Relaxation Technique 4

- Lie or sit with your eyes closed. Count 10 outward breaths. Visualise yourself walking through a meadow by a stream in the sunshine. Be aware of all the sounds and feelings or your visualisation. Fly above the scene as a bird or butterfly. As thoughts come to your mind let them form into small white clouds and float away.

Relaxation Technique 5

- Watch the second hand on a watch or clock and count how many breaths you take in 10 seconds. In the next 10 seconds, and without holding your breath, try to breath deeper and reduce the number of breaths

6. Working with avoidance

Children who have experienced child sexual assault sometimes develop coping strategies to enable day-to-day functioning. For example they detach from the emotional and physical pain of events, especially when abuse continues over a long period of time. Typical avoidance strategies employed by children include: denial, forgetting (repressing memories), dissociation and displacement.

Here is an activity you may consider utilising when counselling a client who is using avoidance as a coping mechanism.

1. Avoidance Homework.

The aim of this technique is to encourage clients to face fears that are interrupting their everyday life.

Avoidance Activity 1: Avoidance Homework

Age group: 6–14+ years

Instructions: Explanation to child

1. Explain to the child that we are going to look at some of the things you are scared of and try to work on little steps to help you not be scared of these anymore.

Directions

1. Talk with the child about the fear and why they are scared of the thing/situation.
2. Help the child to think up a number of small steps that would lead to them overcoming their fear.
3. Make up a chart with the child (like a behaviour chart) that rewards them for each day that they achieve the step for that week. For example, if a child will not sleep on their own, the first step may be to have a mattress on the floor in their parents' bedroom, the next week might be for them to have their mattress just outside their parent's door etc. Older children may simply need to be challenged to take a step closer to their fear each week.
4. The same process can be used for any fear and can be broken into a number of steps. If a step becomes very difficult it can be worked on for a number of weeks.

Information for parent/carer

Explain to the parent or carer that you are going to give their child some homework to help them to make steps towards facing a fear. Talk to them about their role in this process.

7. Working with feelings

Helping a child to become in touch with their feelings is very important after a traumatic experience. A very gentle way for a child to communicate their feelings is through art. Invite them to draw a picture of how they are feeling when they suddenly become angry or scared or anxious. Be careful not to interpret what they have drawn, but instead ask questions such as 'Can you tell me what is happening in your picture?' 'You have used the colour yellow a lot, what does that colour mean in your picture?' 'What does that colour feel like in your body?' Remember to thank them for sharing this with you.

Here are seven activities you may consider using when counselling a client to assist them in expressing their emotions in an appropriate way. The techniques are as follows:

1. All My Faces
2. Feelings Book
3. Feelings Dice
4. Feelings Hands
5. Feelings Pictures
6. Hot Potato Game
7. My Special Journal.

The aim of the following techniques is to enable the child or young person to feel better equipped to identify and express their feelings. These therapeutic strategies may aid the client to examine, externalise and eventually reduce negative feelings such as excessive anger.

Feelings Activity 1: All My Faces

Age group: 5–10 years

Materials

- paper
- pens, pencils, crayons or textas

Instructions: Explanation to child

1. 'We are going to draw four faces. The faces are happy, sad, angry and scared. I would like for you to draw a face for each feeling and tell me about a time when you felt like that.'

Directions

1. Ask the child to draw a happy face and talk about a time when they felt happy. Write what they say at the top of the face.
2. Ask the child to draw a sad face and talk about a time when they felt sad. Write what they say at the top of the face.
3. Ask the child to draw a scared face and talk about a time when they felt scared. Write what they say at the top of the face.
4. Ask the child to draw an angry face and talk about a time when they felt angry. Write what they say at the top of the face.

Notes

Younger children might like to use facial expressions instead. They may need help to write above the face.

Feelings Activity 2: Feelings Book

Age group: 6–10 years

Materials

- paper
- pens, pencils, crayons or textas
- stapler

Instructions: Explanation to child

1. 'We are going to talk about a feeling and describe what colour it is, and then make a book.'

Directions

1. Ask the child to tell you about a feeling.
2. Ask the child what colour they might picture this feeling to be.
3. Paint a piece of paper in that colour.
4. When the paint has dried, ask the child to write the feeling at the top of the page.
5. Using the outline of the gingerbread man (below), ask the child to draw what that feeling looks like and where in the body the feeling is felt.
6. At the bottom of the page ask the child to write about a time they felt like this.
7. Repeat the process with the other colours and feelings
8. Make a cover for the book and staple the pages in.

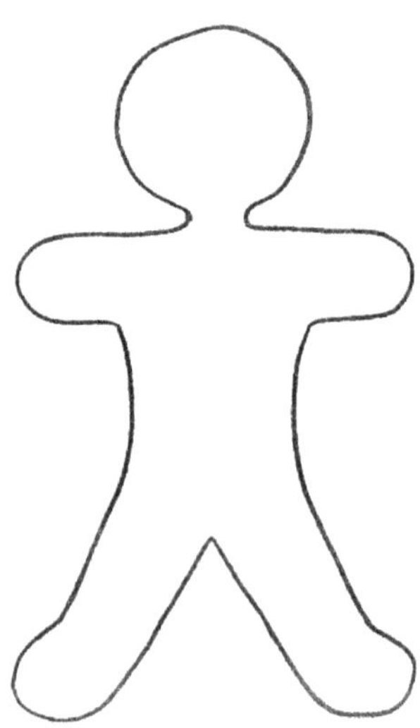

Feelings Activity 3: Feelings Dice

Age group: 6–10 years

Materials

- cardboard
- pictures from magazines or cards
- glue

Instructions: Explanation to child

1. 'We are going to play a game where we roll the dice and whatever side is face up is the side that we talk about.'

Directions

1. Collect pictures that represent children showing a variety of emotions.
2. Make a cube out of cardboard.
3. Glue the pictures on the sides of the dice.
4. Take turns rolling the dice. Encourage the child to talk to you about the emotion/feeling that is represented. If they are having difficulties offer them suggestions.

Notes

Younger children may prefer to use facial expressions and talk about a time when they felt that feeling.

Feelings Activity 4: Feelings Hands

Age group: 5–10 years

Materials

- paper
- pens or textas

Instructions: Explanation to child

1. 'There are sometimes a lot of things that we like and don't like. Today I thought that we might put those things on to the hands that we have drawn.'

Directions

1. Draw an outline of two hands on A4 paper.
2. On one hand the child identifies five things that they like.
3. On the other hand the child identifies five things that they don't like.

Notes

Younger children might need help to write the things down on the hands.

Feelings Activity 5: Feelings Pictures

Age group: 5–14+ years

Materials

- paper
- pens, textas, paint, crayons
- craft items such as glitter, sand, ribbon, etc.
- glue

Instructions: Explanation to child

1. 'Sometimes when something bad has happened to someone they can be left with lots of different feelings. We are going to try and explore those feelings by drawing and painting.'

Directions

1. Explain that you can start with a person outline or a heart shape or just a blank piece of paper. You can help the child draw these if necessary.
2. Provide the child with paint, textas, pastels and other items such as glitter, sand, and ribbon.
3. Ask the child to show you on the paper how they are feeling inside.
4. If the picture is very dark and angry then it is a good idea, if the child is willing, to follow this with a picture of what they would like their feelings to look like in the future.
5. Explore with the child what the different colours and shapes etc. represent within their pictures.

Notes

Older children may choose to use words or draw symbols to represent the things currently going on in their life or what they want for the future.

Feelings Activity 6: Hot Potato Game

Age group: 5–10 years

Materials

- toy stuffing
- old brown stocking
- feeling tokens (or stickers with faces expressing different feelings)
- CD player and music

Instructions: Explanation to child

1. 'Whenever the music stops, whoever is holding the potato has to show the other person a sad, happy, angry or scared face and if you want you can talk about a time when you felt like that.'

Directions

1. Make a fake hot potato by stuffing an old brown stocking.
2. Pass the potato back and forth until the music stops.
3. Whoever is holding the potato picks up a feelings token and talks about that feeling.

Notes

Children aged 6 to 10 years may want to use scenario cards.

Be aware that this activity involves self-disclosure on the therapist's part, and the practitioner must remain mindful of using appropriate personal examples that do not burden or trigger the child in any way.

Feelings Activity 7: My Special Journal

Age group: 6–10+ years

Materials

- exercise book
- pens, textas, paint, crayons
- craft items such as glitter, ribbon

Instructions: Explanation to child

1. 'This book will be your special book to use everyday where you can write or draw whatever you are feeling.'
2. 'If you like you can bring it to your session and we can talk about it.'

Directions

1. Ask the child to decorate an exercise book. This book will be their special book that is only for them.
2. Ask the child to take the book home and each day write or draw a picture of how they are feeling or what they are thinking.
3. They might like to include a special photo or picture that is important to them.
4. Encourage the child to bring the journal with them to the sessions.

Information for parent/carer

Let the parent or carer know that their child has made a book to help explore and express feelings. It is a private book she/he may show others what is written but no one is to look in the book without permission.

8. Working with negative self-thoughts

Children who have been sexually assaulted commonly present negative thoughts and statements about themselves that become the child's pervasive internalised view of themselves and of external situations. Negative thoughts are often related to low self-esteem, guilt, embarrassment and self-blame

Here are three activities you may consider using when counselling a client who is experiencing negative thoughts. The techniques are as follows:

1. Events Diary
2. The Pits — Part 1
3. The Pits — Part 2.

The aim of the following techniques is to assist your client to become aware of, and change, negative thought patterns. They may assist the child or young person to examine, externalise and eventually reduce feelings and expressions of depression and negative thought patterns.

Negative Thoughts Activity 1: Events Diary

Age group: 5–14+ years

Materials

- exercise book
- pens, textas, paint, crayons
- craft items such as glitter and ribbon

Instructions: Explanation to child

1. 'We are going to decorate an events diary for you to take home and use. An events diary is a book that you can write or draw in about different events, good or bad, that happen during your day.'
2. 'Then you can bring your events diary with you to counselling each week and we can talk about it.'
3. 'First, we are going to decorate your events diary so it is your special book.'

Directions

1. Using an exercise book, assist the child to cover their events diary with plain or patterned paper.
2. Then assist the child to decorate their events diary.
3. Explain to the child that it is a good idea to write the date or day at the top of each page before writing or drawing about the events of that day in their diary. Give them an example of what they could write or draw about.
4. Explain to the child (and their caregiver) that their events diary is their own private book and they do not have to show its contents to anyone unless they choose to do so.
5. Ask the child to bring their events book back to the next counselling session with them.

Information for parent/carer

Ask caregivers of younger clients to encourage or even assist their children to add entries to their events book each day.

Notes

Older children may prefer to use a hard-covered book for this activity.

Negative Thoughts Activity 2: The Pits — Part One

Important note

The Pits Part 1 must be followed by The Pits Part 2 during the same session.

Age group: 11–14+ years

Materials

- paper
- pens, textas or crayons
- plastic contact

Instructions: Explanation to young person

1. 'We are going to think about all of the people, situations and beliefs that have contributed to you feeling so negative about your self and your life.'
2. Explain that often as these 'bad' things happen we feel lower and lower until we feel we are stuck at the bottom of a pit.
3. Check that the young person can relate to this idea.

Directions

1. Draw for the young person or ask them to draw a picture of their pit with them at the bottom.
2. On one side of the pit write out all the people or situations that have had a negative influence on the young person through their life (back to when the negative or depressed feelings began).
3. On the other side write how each of these people or situations have impacted on the young person and what they have believed about themselves or their life as a result.
4. Discuss why the people acted so negatively towards the young person (e.g., for their own feelings of power/to share their own hurt).
5. If the young person is suicidal, discuss how taking their own life will mean that these people will have won.

Negative Thoughts Activity 3: The Pits — Part Two

Important note

The Pits Part 2 must follow The Pits Part 1 during the same session.

Age group: 11–14+ years

Materials

- paper
- pens, textas or crayons
- plastic contact

Instructions: Explanation to young person

1. 'We are now going to think about all the things you are going to need to do and believe in order to climb out of the pit.'
2. 'At the top we are going to draw all the people who will help you with this.'

Directions

1. Draw for the young person or ask them to draw a picture of their pit with them on a ladder climbing out.
2. On one side of the pit write out all the things that the young person is going to have to do or believe to get out of the pit.
3. On the other side write what difference these things will make and what impact they will have.
4. Discuss any fears the young person may have about the fact that they will be 'different' when they are no longer feeling depressed/negative.
5. Young people sometimes feel more comfortable where they are as it is familiar, they may feel that the depression is a large part of who they are, so this exercise may be challenging for them.

9. Working with self-esteem

Low self-esteem is common amongst children who have been sexually assaulted. Children may experience low self-esteem as a constant feeling of worthlessness, repetitive voices telling them they are not good enough, or feelings that they do not deserve to feel happy or experience good things.

Here are six activities you may consider using to help build your client's self-esteem. The techniques are as follows:

1. Book About Me
2. Feel Good Jar
3. 'I Can' Poster
4. Special Keepsake Box
5. Life-Sized Poster of Self
6. Life-Sized Hero Poster.

The aim of the following techniques is to increase the child's self-esteem and raise their self-awareness of their abilities, strengths, resources and resilience.

Self-Esteem Activity 1: Book About Me

Age group: 5–14+ years

Materials

- A3 paper
- old magazines
- pens, pencils or crayons
- craft items such as glitter and stickers
- glue

Instructions: Explanation to child

1. 'We are going to make a book all about you.'
2. 'We can write and draw, or create a collage about your family and friends, your favourite things, things that make you happy and things that make you sad.'

Directions

1. Help your client create a 'Book About Me' and work through the pages with the child one by one.
2. Use 6 sheets of A3 paper folded in half to create a book
3. Ask the child if they wish to decorate the front page of their book with stickers.
4. Put headings on each page and ask the child to write, draw or make a collage for each page of the book; for example:
   - 'This is Me and My Family' — the child might draw or write phrases to describe themselves and their family members
   - 'My Favourite Things' — ask the child if they would like to make a collage of their favourite things on this page.
   - 'I am Sad When' and 'I am Happy When' pages are a good opportunity to explore with the child the things that make them feel happy or sad, and why this is so.
5. After completion of the book ask the child if you can photocopy their book, and add it to the child's file.

Information for parent/carer

Talk with the parent or carer about how creating this book allows for discussion and expanding of each of the above mentioned areas.

Notes

Older children may wish to place a photo of themselves on the 'This is Me' page. They may also wish to create a family tree, rather than draw pictures of their family members.

Self-Esteem Activity 2: Feel Good Jar

Age group: 6–14+ years

Materials

- jar
- plastic sleeve
- window paint
- coloured paper

Instructions: Explanation to child

1. 'We are going to decorate a "feel good jar" for you too take home and fill with good things about yourself.'
2. 'On the pieces of coloured paper write one good thing about yourself each day and place it in your feel good jar.'
3. 'Then I want you to bring your jar back to your next session so we talk about all of these good things.'

Directions

1. Using window paints create drawings/decorations on a plastic sleeve.
2. While drawing, explain to the child what self-esteem is and the benefits of high self-esteem rather than low self-esteem.
3. Discuss with child examples of what they could write about themselves to place in their jar (e.g., 'I am a good friend')
4. The child can take the drawings/decorations home on the plastic sleeve and when they are dry, place them on the jar.
5. Give the child coloured pieces of paper to take home to write 'good things about themselves' each day and add to their jar.
6. Ask the child (and caregiver) to bring their feel good jar back to the next session.
7. At the next session talk with child about their self-esteem and discuss what they have written about themselves on their pieces of paper.
8. Ask the child how has this exercise affected how they feel about themselves? Have they learnt anything new about themselves?

9. Explain to the child that as he/she fills their feel good jar and learns that there are more and more good things about themselves their self-esteem will also increase.

Information for parent/carer

Suggest that the caregiver (and other family members) could also write some positive things about the child and, with the child's permission, add them to the child's 'feel good jar'.

Notes

It may be beneficial to use a plastic rather than glass jar with the 6- to 10-year age group.

Self-Esteem Activity 3: 'I Can' Poster

Age group: 6–10 years

Materials

- 'I Can Monsters'/'Can Do Dinosaurs' cards
- A3 paper
- pens, textas or crayons

Instructions: Explanation to child

1. 'We are going to use the 'I Can Monsters'/'Can Do Dinosaurs' cards (see reference below).'
2. 'By using these cards we are going to find all the things that you can do.'
3. 'I also thought it would be a great idea if we make all the things that you can do into a poster.'

Directions

1. Using the 'I Can Monsters'/'Can Do Dinosaurs' cards, show each of the cards to the child.
2. Place the cards that the child believes they can do to one side. These cards are the YES 'I Can' cards.
3. After you have gone through all of the pack, show the YES cards again to the child and ask them to tell you about a time when they were able to do this; for example, 'I can be brave when I sleep with the light off'.
4. Ask the child to write or draw the situation on the poster.

Notes

The 'I Can Monsters'/'Can Do Dinosaurs' cards and the 'Strength Cards for Kids' are from St Luke's Innovative Resources — for more information see the following website: www.innovativeresources.org

Older children may find the strength cards more suitable.

Self-Esteem Activity 4: Special Keepsake Box

Age group: 5–14+ years

Materials

- shoe box
- coloured paper/gift-wrapping paper
- textas
- miscellaneous craft items (eg. glitter, feathers, stickers, etc.)

Instructions: Explanation to child

1. 'We are going to make a special keepsake box for you to keep special things in to remind you of good memories and to remind you that you are a special person.'

Directions

1. Using a box with a lid, help the child to decorate their special keepsake box in anyway that they choose.
2. Encourage the child that it is their special keepsake box and will be one of a kind just like they are.
3. Discuss some of the special things that the child can keep in their special keepsake box, such as nice letters and cards from friends and family, photos, postcards from fun places that they have been to, or anything else that helps them to feel good about themselves.
4. This is a good opportunity to write a quick letter to your client, letting them know the good qualities you see in them and give it to them to start of their collection in their special keepsake box.
5. Explain to the child that their special keepsake box is private and therefore they don't have to share its contents with others, unless they choose to.
6. The child's special keepsake box can be used at any time to remind the child of how special they are.

Information for parent/carer

Ask the child's family members (if appropriate) to also write a letter or card expressing what they appreciate about the child.

Explain to the parent or carer that their child's special keepsake box is private and therefore they don't have to share its contents with others, unless they choose to.

Self-Esteem Activity 5: Life-Sized Poster of Self

Age group: 5–13 years

Materials

- butcher's paper
- textas, paint
- craft material such as wool, beads glitter, feathers, stickers
- glue

Instructions: Explanation to child

1. 'We are going to create a life sized poster of you.'

Directions

1. Let the child know that you are going to help them create a life-sized poster of him/herself.
2. Ask the child if they feel comfortable to lie down on a big piece of paper so you can draw around their body outline. If the child feels uncomfortable to lie down, they may feel more comfortable to stand in front of the paper, against the wall. Let the child know that they can ask you to stop at any time.
3. Draw around the child's body outline (be careful not to draw close to the child's private areas, these areas of the outline can be drawn freehand later).
4. Help the child to create a poster with a face, hair, clothes, shoes, jewellery and so on, so that it resembles them. They may wish to draw the clothes they are in or their best party clothes or clothes they would like to have. Paint or fabric can be used. Real beads can be used for the jewellery.
5. Explain to the child that you are now going write things about them all over the poster, such as things they like, things they do not like, things that they are good at doing (use Strength Cards if child is struggling to think of things that they are good at doing) and details about them (e.g., hair colour, eye colour).

Information for parent/carer

This activity may take more than one session. In between sessions get the child's caregivers to help them think of good things about themselves and ask them to get suggestions from other people in the child's life. If the suggestions are written down then pockets can be added to the picture to store these in so the child can keep them.

Notes

The 'Strength Cards for Kids' are from St Luke's Innovative Resources — for more information see the following website: www.innovativeresources.org

Self-Esteem Activity 6: Life-Sized Hero Poster

(This is similar to the Superhero Self in the section on Fear; however, the aim of the following technique is to increase self-esteem, rather than reduce fear).

Age group: 5–13 years

Materials

- butcher's paper
- textas, paint
- craft material such as wool, beads glitter, feathers, stickers
- glue

Instructions: Explanation to child

1. 'We are going to create a life-sized poster of you as your favourite hero.'

Directions

1. Ask the child who their hero is and what it is that makes this person/ character their hero.
2. Let the child know that you are going to help them create a life-sized poster of him/her as their hero.
3. Ask the child if they feel comfortable to lie down on a big piece of paper so you can draw around their body outline. If the child feels uncomfortable to lie down, they may feel more comfortable to stand in front of the paper, against the wall.
4. Draw around the child's body outline (be careful not to draw close to the child's private areas; these areas of the outline can be drawn freehand later).
5. Ask the child what this person/character does that makes them a hero and does the child do any of these things (e.g., helps others)?

Notes

The child may prefer to be drawn as a fairy, princess or knight. Discuss with the child the virtues and powers of their chosen character and why they would like to be like this.

10. Working with Self-blame and Responsibility

Due to the personal nature of child sexual assault and because these experiences often occur within already established relationships, the child can take on responsibility and blame themselves for the assault. Often the grooming techniques used, as well as the powerful dynamics between the adult and the child, leads to feelings of guilt and shame that can have adverse affects for the child's self-image and development.

Here is an activity you may consider using when counselling a client who is possibly internalising blame and responsibility following sexual assault:

1. Paper Dolls.

The aim of this activity is to assess the child's perception of victimisation, responsibility and blame. It also assists the child to develop a sense of family and community support.

Blame & Responsibility Activity 1: Paper Dolls

(Source: Crisci, G., Lay M., & Lowenstein, L. (1998). *Paper dolls and paper airplanes: therapeutic exercises for sexually traumatized children.* Toronto: Champion Press.)

Age group: All ages

Materials

- paper
- scissors
- pens, pencils
- stickers (happy faces, dots, stars)
- band-aids

Instructions: Explanation to child

1. With reference to the sexual assault, explain to the child that you are going to do an activity called paper dolls.
2. Explain to the child that the purpose of this activity is for them to show you how they, and others, may feel about what happened to them.

Directions

1. To make a string of eight paper dolls (note that for younger children, counsellors may need to pre-cut paper dolls):
   - Using clear tape, tape both sides of the shorter ends of two sheets of paper to make a long piece of paper.
   - Fold the paper from end to end in half, then in half again and in half a third time.
   - Cut out the pattern of the paper doll (at the end of this activity) and place the pattern on the folded paper so that the ends of the hands are touching the creases of the paper. Trace the dolls outline onto the paper.
   - Cut along the outline for the doll (but do not cut along the creases where the hands touch the ends of the paper).
   - Gently pull open the folds and spread out the chain of paper dolls.
2. School-aged children:
   - Once the paper dolls have been made, instruct the child to label each doll by writing the names of the people who are important to them (include themselves, parents, siblings, and the person who sexually assaulted them as well as other family members/carers, friends, school teachers and so on).

- Give the child 10 band-aids and 10 of each of the three stickers (dots, stars and happy faces).
- Ask the child to use the stickers to show how they feel about the people in their life.
- Ask the child to put band-aids on those people hurt because of the sexual assault (they can place as many or as few band-aids on each person depending on the level of hurt). They can choose how many, if any, band-aids they want to use.
- Ask the child to put dots on the people they think are to blame for the sexual assault. Use as many dots as required to demonstrate the blame, as few or as many dolls as they like.
- Place stars on the people that they child thinks are brave.
- Place happy faces stickers on the people who they know are not to blame for what happened.

3. Preschool-aged children:
   - Provide the child with a string of three paper dolls (pre-cut). Label each doll (one for child, one for abuser and one for parent / caregiver).
   - Guide the child in using the stickers by saying:

     'These band-aids are for hurt, like when you feel sad. Put a band-aid on the person who you think is feeling hurt or sad because of the secret touching. You can put just one band-aid if you think that person is a little bit hurt, or you can put lots of band-aids if you think the person is feeling a lot of hurt. If there is anyone else who you think is feeling hurt, you can put band-aids on that person too. Now put the dots on the person who is to blame for the secret touching.'
   - Be sure to explain that blame means whose fault it is, and give an example of blame to ensure the children understand what the concept means.

     'Put happy faces on anyone who knows you are not to blame for the secret touching. The stars are for bravery. Bravery means doing something that is really hard to do, like swimming in the deep end of the pool for the first time. Put the stars on the person/s who are brave.'

Notes

This activity serves as a useful assessment tool as it assists children to visually express their understanding of the assault and associated blame, responsibility and support. Where the child has a skewed perception of the responsibility, this can form the basis of a case plan to work with the children in more detail. Remember, this is an exploratory tool for the counsellor to explore why the child may feel like they do, not to correct their view by telling them how they should feel.

Where appropriate ask the client if they would like to cut or rearrange the dolls as part of the activity. You may then want to revisit this activity at a later date to see whether the client's feelings have changed during the counselling process.

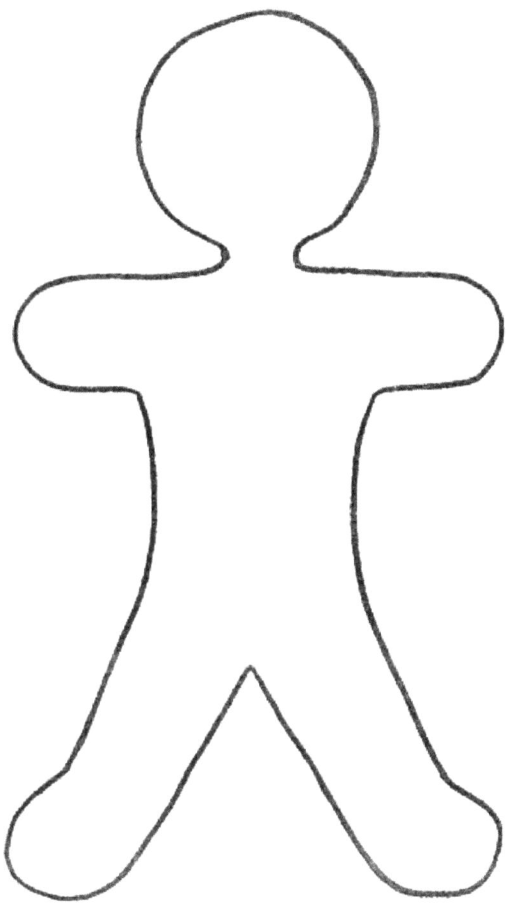

Chapter 4: Review questions

Choose one or two interventions that you think may be appropriate for one of your clients.

1. How would you introduce this activity to the child in the session? What language would you use?
2. How would you respond if the child disclosed sexual assault during this activity? What language would you use?
3. If the child did not seem engaged in the activity how would you approach this with them?
4. How would you introduce the client's parents/family to these activities? What risks/benefits might there be to involving the family in this process?
5. Try completing one or two activities as if you were the client. Reflect on the process of completing the activity. How did you feel whilst you were engaged in the activity?
6. Role play with your colleagues and/or supervisor. Take turns being the client and the therapist. Reflect on the process. What was effective? What could have been improved? How did the client engage/respond? What was their feedback on this process? Did anything occur unexpectedly? If so, how did you manage this?

Chapter 5

Psycho-Educational Tools: Teaching Personal Safety

The aim of this chapter is to give practitioners the knowledge and skills to assist parents and caregivers to understand the nature of normal sexual development in children and introduce Bravehearts' psycho-educational personal safety program.

Chapter overview

1. Understanding normal and problematic sexual development in children.
2. Reducing problematic sexual behaviour in children.
3. Introduction to Bravehearts' Personal Safety education as part of a holistic response to child sexual assault.

Upon completion of this chapter it is intended that you:

1. will be able to assist parents and caregivers to understand the nature of normal sexual development and how to respond to problematic sexualised behaviours
2. have an increased ability to deliver psycho-educational personal safety strategies as part of a holistic therapeutic response.

Sexual development in children: Healthy and unhealthy behaviours

Just as language acquisition, motor development, and cognitive development are a natural part of growth and learning in children, so too is sexual development. Although children are not 'sexual' beings in the way adult sexuality is seen, they do go through a number of different stages of sexual development, most of which are a natural and healthy part of growing up and learning about their bodies and their world.

Young children (2–5 years) may exhibit some sexual behaviours that would be considered very unusual in children over the ages of 6, such as putting their mouth on their mother's breast or playing with themselves in public. The reason these behaviours tend to reduce when children reach approximately 6 years of age is due to a combination of their developmental stage and socialisation effects.

Natural and healthy sexual exploration by children is an information-gathering process, whereby children explore each other's bodies by looking and touching (like playing doctor) and also explore gender roles (like playing house), with the vast majority of children engaging in these behaviours at different developmental points in childhood. Characteristics of normal and healthy sexual development include:

- When this exploration is with children of a similar age, developmental status and participation is voluntary, this can be considered natural and healthy sexual exploration.
- Although siblings engage in mutual exploration, mostly this exploration is between children who have an existing friendship.
- The sexual play occurs over several periods in child's development, and is limited in type and frequency.
- Curiosity in sex and sexuality is also balanced with curiosity about other aspects of their life
- Children often feel embarrassment, but not usually feelings of shame, fear, anxiety or anger about the sexual exploration.
- If and when children are discovered in an act of sexual exploration by adults and they are instructed to stop and their behaviour is monitored, this behaviour most often diminishes.

Sexual behaviours common in all children include:

- trying to look at people who are naked
- touching own private parts in private
- interest in opposite sex
- masturbation.

Common sexual behaviours in children between the ages of 3 to 5 years and uncommon in children 6 years and over include:

- touching mum's breasts
- touching own private parts in front of others
- standing too close to people
- kissing other children
- showing private parts to same-age peers.

Sexual behaviours uncommon in children of any age include:

- masturbation with an object (doll, hair brush, chair)
- trying to have intercourse with others
- touching animals' private parts
- drawing pictures of private parts
- asking others to do sexual acts on them
- pretending toys are having sex
- placing objects in the anus or vagina.

Characteristics of problematic sexual behaviours:

- Children engaged in the behaviours don't have an ongoing friendship — as sexual play is usually an extension of regular play behaviour.
- Sexual behaviours are engaged in with children younger or older than the child — generally the wider the age gap the larger the concern
- Children have too much knowledge about sexuality than would be expected of their age — when children have been exposed to explicit adult sexuality, pornography, poor boundaries, or sexual assault they may display sexual knowledge beyond their years.

- Sexual behaviours continue in spite of clear, consistent requests to stop — when these behaviours continue despite parental requests to stop or even in the face of punishment, the behaviours may be a conscious or unconscious method of indicating the child needs help.

Reducing problematic sexualised behaviours

It is very important when trying to reduce sexualised behaviours in children not to make the child feel ashamed of their behaviours. Negative comments such as 'That is disgusting' or 'Don't be a dirty boy/girl' can cause a child to feel that they are disgusting or dirty, which can compound the problem. When working to reduce problematic sexualised behaviours, be sure to remain consistent and use a calm tone of voice. It is important to convey to the child that they are not in trouble for their actions, but that you wish them to stop what they are doing.

To reduce these behaviours, it is recommended that parents:

1. address behaviour in a short, direct but calm way — for example, 'No touching privates', 'Hands out of pants'.
2. redirect behaviour — 'Would you like to play with your doll here, or your blocks?' or
3. distract — 'Let's go read a book together hey?' 'Come up here and see what mum's making for dinner', 'Come up here and let's colour in'.
4. praise good behaviour — remember to PRAISE their child when they are NOT displaying sexualised behaviours, so they also receive attention for good behaviour.
5. set long term boundaries — ensure that consistent boundaries are in place in relation to what is appropriate.

Personal safety education: Part of an holistic response to sexual assault

Keeping children safe is one of the most important roles of parents, educators, or other caring adults. To do this, children must be equipped with the knowledge and skills they need to avoid risky situations, and an understanding of their rights to protect their own body.

Teaching children personal safety helps them learn the skills to identify their vulnerabilities, while devising strategies to both protect themselves and get help if unable to cope alone. While talking to children about sexual assault may prompt parental discomfort, personal safety can and should be taught to all children —

even preschoolers. Thankfully, very young children can be taught personal safety without ever hearing frightening terms like 'sexual assault'.

As a holistic approach to combating child sexual assault in the community, Bravehearts' Education and Prevention stream currently includes the following strategies.

1. The 'Ditto's Keep Safe Adventure' CD-Rom and associated products

Heightened media coverage has ensured parents and caregivers are more aware of the threat to children by sex offenders. The community has learned a lot, including how devastating child sexual assault can be to the health of children. This increased awareness has alarmed many families as they grapple with finding ways to protect their children. In response to this need Bravehearts has created an interactive CD-Rom, 'Ditto's Keep Safe Adventure', with assistance and advice from the best minds in child protection around the nation and featuring our children's character Ditto.

Other products based on the CD-Rom that have been developed and are available include an Activity book, 'Ditto's Keep Safe Adventure Show!' DVD, and a CD of five 'Ditto's Keep Safe Adventure Songs'. The Ditto CD-Rom and associated products are available for purchase from our website: www.bravehearts.org.au.

Bravehearts' therapists utilise the Ditto's Keep Safe Adventure CD-Rom and Workbook in the counselling room. These resources allow the therapist to deliver age-appropriate messages regarding personal safety and at no point mention sex or sexual assault. The CD-Rom and Workbook cover topics including: private parts, what private means, rules about touching, secrets, trusting instincts and who to tell if you feel unsafe.

These resources provide the foundation for the psycho-educational component of the therapists' case plan. For example, if the therapist sees a particular client for six to eight sessions, they may spend two or three sessions working through the Ditto personal safety program together. The program can be used on its own, or integrated into a client's overall case plan. This psycho-educational program is available to organisations external to Bravehearts. However, therapists must be mindful of the vulnerability of this client group, and the importance of providing a holistic response to this issue, including the participation of parents in the program, when considering its implementation.

Parents and carers are encouraged to consolidate the personal safety information by revisiting the CD-Rom or Workbook alongside their child on a regular basis in the home environment. Advise parents that teaching children personal safety is similar to teaching them road rules or how to swim: it is not something you talk to them about on a single occasion, but rather a topic when can be revisited and consolidated on a regular basis with their child, to reinforce the key messages.

2. The 'Ditto's Keep Safe Adventure' interactive school-based program

The purpose of the Ditto's Keep Safe Adventure Education Program is to teach children the skills to keep safe from sexual predators. We are taking the proven, safe, fun, effective and interactive messages, rules and tools in our interactive CD-Rom, Ditto's Keep Safe Adventure, into schools, day care centres, shopping centres, sporting clubs etc in order to provide children, parents, teachers, carers and the general community with specialised child sexual assault awareness and education.

The live protective behaviour performance runs for 30 minutes. The star of the performance is Bravehearts' mascot Ditto. The program is fun, non-threatening and encourages student participation through interaction and song. Segments include:

- Yes and No feelings
- Your body's warning signs
- Scared and yucky feelings
- Private parts
- It's OK to say NO if you don't feel safe
- Secrets
- What to do if you feel unsafe or unsure

The following comment is from a family member, following a disclosure made by their nephew, which was a result of seeing 'Ditto's Keep Safe Adventure' at school.

> *... a huge thank you to this organisation. Yesterday I found out that my nephews were the victims of a vicious child predator. They are young and very vulnerable. They were compelled to come forward with this information after keeping it a secret for many months, after attending the program run through their school. I dread to think, had it not been for this, that we would have been none the wiser ... so thank you on behalf of these children and their parents. You may have just saved their lives!*

Chapter 5: Review questions

1. List five of the examples of healthy sexual exploration in children preschool-aged children?
2. How would you advise a parent who is concerned about their 5-year-old's repeated and constant sexualised behaviour?
3. Why is it important for there to be an holistic approach to prevention that includes adult education and awareness as well as programs aimed at children and young people?
4. What would you teach a young child to protect them against sexual assault?
5. If you were to present to a high school class, what information would you consider important for them to know to protect themselves?

Chapter 6

The Toll on the Therapist

The aim of this chapter is to highlight for practitioners the importance of both self-care and organisational-care, neither of which can be underestimated, when working in the area of sexual assault. As such, this chapter is focused on increasing the awareness of the symptoms of vicarious trauma and to introduce relevant self- and organisational-care strategies that may assist in preventing vicarious trauma, and burnout.

Chapter overview

1. Identifying vicarious trauma.
2. The importance of organisational-care and self-care.

Upon completion of this chapter it is intended that you will:

1. have a comprehensive understanding of the identifiers of vicarious trauma
2. have an understanding of the importance of organisational-care and self-care and be able to implement these care strategies in your workplace setting.

Vicarious trauma

Vicarious trauma is defined as 'the transformation that occurs in the inner experience of the therapist (or other professional) that comes about as a result of empathic engagement with clients' (Pearlman & Saakvitne, as cited in Morrison 2007, p. 2).

It is pertinent to note here that vicarious trauma is a normal response to repeated exposure to traumatic material. It happens to many professionals, whether it is discussed openly or not. It can have a cumulative effect that permeates all areas of an individual's professional and personal life. It can effect every organisation that works within the trauma field and must be addressed openly and effectively within each organisation.

Often the experience of vicarious trauma is synonymous with those symptoms experienced by the primary victim. Research suggests that it is the amount of exposure to traumatic material, over and above anything else that best predicts vicarious traumatisation.

> *Counsellors must personally endure repeated exposure to distress and use their own feelings of sorrow as tools for therapy. As such, it is impossible to escape this kind of work without personal consequences. (Campbell, as cited in Morrison, 2007, p. 5.)*

Common symptoms associated with vicarious trauma may include, but are not limited to:

- physiological (e.g., heart palpitations, headaches, difficulty concentrating);
- intrusive reactions (e.g., nightmares, flashbacks, obsessive thoughts);
- hypervigilance
- burnout
- counter-transference
- anxiety and/or depression
- feeling overwhelming emotions (e.g., anger, shame, guilt)
- irritability
- procrastination
- feelings of reduced personal and professional accomplishment
- low self-esteem
- loss of energy

- sleep disturbance
- increased feelings of cynicism
- increased sensitivity to violence (direct, indirect)
- profound distrust of others
- interpersonal relationship breakdown
- substance misuse
- feelings of vulnerability

Vicarious trauma can also lead to a change in an individual's 'cognitive schema' (beliefs about the world, self and others; Morrison, 2007). This can lead to feelings of distrust, that the world is no longer 'safe'; and of helplessness and disempowerment.

At an organisational level, vicarious trauma can manifest in 're-enactment of client issues' (Morrison, 2007, p. 3). Examples include betrayal and distrust among workers, secrecy and boundary violations, reduced employee health, reduced work efficacy and job satisfaction, staff turnover, reduced quality of client care, increased levels of absenteeism, sick leave and workers compensation and at times over identification with the work (Morrison, 2007).

This can spill over into the individual's personal life leading to conflict and dissatisfaction in relationships with family and friends (Morrison, 2007).

Due to the nature of this work, media-fuelled stereotypes and hype can exacerbate symptoms, as individuals become alienated and feel they can not express their feelings freely. To further compound these feelings, issues such as lack of funding, political responses and associated feelings of frustration with the 'system' can result in individuals becoming emotionally overwhelmed and exhausted.

Research suggests that the issue of vicarious trauma is most prominent among workers in the field of sexual assault.

Professionals working with children and young people who have experienced sexual assault, repeatedly witness trauma that is not benign to their own bodies and minds.

Minimising vicarious trauma

Historically, the prevention of vicarious trauma and burnout in professionals was linked to individual coping strategies and resilience levels in workers (Morrison, 2007). However, recent research suggests that this focus not only places unwarranted responsibility and blame on the worker, it inadvertently denies the importance of the organisation and the ecosystemic context within which professionals work and live. As such, this section will address all three contexts when recommending ways to prevent, or at least reduce, individual experience's of vicarious trauma:

Individual level

Pearlman & Saakvitne (1995) suggest that to minimise vicarious trauma you should know, and practise, your A-B-Cs :

Awareness

Take the time to self-reflect. It is important to be attuned to your needs, limits, emotions and resources.

Balance

Maintaining healthy boundaries and balance among work, home and play. Maintaining inner balance is essential. As is, learning to relax to maximise physical and emotional health.

Connection

Connectedness to oneself, to others and to something larger (e.g., spiritual) is important to offset feelings of isolation and increase validation and hope.

Bayliss (2008) suggests the following:

- Clearly setting boundaries of 'their time' and 'my time' is an important step to regaining control over your life. Creating time for rest and leisure is part of this. Finding activities that focus your mind and body elsewhere, such as reading, bushwalking, sports, gardening, or playing with children, aid in clearly separating work time from leisure.
- Maintain a positive view of the world. When working with clients who have experienced trauma, it may become easy to believe that the world is falling apart or that people are going mad. The world is not falling apart everywhere and not everyone is mad. Remember that, although bad things happen and people are affected, there is a lot of good that goes on as well. Work to look for the good in people and situations. Remember the good you are doing. We are working with a minority of people the majority of the time!

- Have you done the best you can under the circumstances? It is easy to become obsessed with what we might, should, or could have done. Focusing on doing good work and learning from mistakes is an important part of growing as a professional. If you have done the best you could with the information you had to work with, let it go and move on to the next thing.
- Do you have realistic expectations of yourself and others? Oftentimes, helping professionals have unrealistically high expectations of themselves and those around them. You can't be with your clients 24 hours a day, 7 days a week. You can't make decisions for them or help them carry out those decisions. Consider the two competing pressures that are part of your job: In one respect, you are expected to be empathic (which requires you to take feelings into consideration), yet on the other hand, you are expected to turn off emotions in order to get a great deal of work done. Knowing that these two expectations are part of your job may help you find a balance. Create reasonable, achievable goals and expectations for yourself and others and see how much better you feel about meeting your expectations!
- The single most important rule to remember as professionals is to balance work and play.

Furthermore, incorporating ways of managing stress into your daily routine will go a long way to making work seem more manageable. There are several ways that you can help yourself re-engage in work activities in a less stressful way:

- First, work to set manageable tasks for yourself. Completing tasks will reduce stress.
- Second, find a pace that works well for you. Some people work better under a deadline while others work better at a slower but well-maintained pace.
- Third, organise your time and activities. Set reasonable goals for yourself and organise your time based on what you need to accomplish in a given day. Be careful not to over-schedule or make long to-do lists that are unreasonable and will only add stress.
- Finally, help someone else. Helping others makes you feel good about yourself. Relationships are an important part of life — rely on them. Giving them up so you can work more deprives yourself of a major stress reliever.

Some other suggestions include:

- healthy eating
- regular exercise as a stress reliever

- allowing for adequate sleep to allow your body to rejuvenate
- practising relaxation techniques (e.g., deep breathing, visual imagery)
- socialising
- spiritual engagement
- engaging in recreational activities (e.g., sport)
- being proactive
- above all, using humour.

The Self-Care Assessment checklist at the end of this chapter is a useful tool for monitoring your self-care.

Organisational level

Organisational support is instrumental to the prevention of vicarious trauma and effective service delivery to clients. Research suggests organisational culture and procedures serve to facilitate or impede opportunity for self-care strategies and routines (Wasco et al., 2002).

Some organisational-care strategies include, but are not limited to:

- allowing for breaks at work, and from work, when needed
- time for debriefing and peer support (formal and informal); this is vital when working in this area. Ensure systemic support is provided at all times.
- ensuring appropriate and diverse caseloads — it is important that there is no pressure to see more than a specified quota due to 'waiting lists' and so on — with mix and match cases, different ages, group versus individual, projects, male/females; and to allow staff multi-level engagement in organisation
- effective professional/clinical supervision; this essential strategy can be delivered in several formats, including group, peer or individual supervision
- provision for leave or paid external supervision for ensuring a balanced work/life or provision for in-house supervision
- allowing staff the opportunity for social interaction between workers (e.g., team building days) to increase workers' sense of support

- safety and comfort in the work environment. There should be policies in place to ensure there is no bullying, threatening or harassment. The workspace should be comfortable, with inspirational material and personal belongings
- allowing flex-time, holidays, time off, continuing education
- making self-care and organisational care part of the organisation's mission statement
- time and allocation of money for self-care activities.

Morrison (2007) suggests that a workplace culture that understands and normalises the effects of working with trauma provides a more stable environment for its workers. It gives permission for workers to take care of themselves.

Ecological level

When thinking about self-care and organisational-care we need to be mindful that workplace policies, legislation and funding will enable, constrain and shape the organisational support structures that can be established in your workplace (Morrison, 2007).

Final note\

We cannot forget the positive impact that individuals in this field make every single day. Among all the traumatic material we witness, we also experience the enormous courage and bravery of individuals affected by sexual assault. At times we are pivotal to the healing process.

Our work extends beyond the individual and permeates all areas of life. This is why we do the work we do and why we endure the hardships of witnessing the pain of others. For this we must in turn be kind to ourselves. We must practise what we preach!

Acknowledgement

The authors gratefully acknowledges that the information contained in this chapter is drawn primarily from Morrison (2007). This article specifically addresses the issue of vicarious trauma within the field of sexual assault.

Self-care assessment

Adapted from Saakvitne, Pearlman, & Staff of TSI/CAAP (1996). *Transforming the pain: A workbook on vicarious traumatisation.* Norton. Retrieved from http://www.ballarat.edu.au/aasp/student/sds/self_care_assess.shtml

The following worksheet for assessing self-care is not exhaustive, merely suggestive. Feel free to add areas of self-care that are relevant for you and rate yourself on how often and how well you are taking care of yourself these days.

When you are finished, look for patterns in your responses. Are you more active in some areas of self-care but ignore others? Are there items on the list that make you think: 'I would never do that'? Listen to your inner responses, your internal dialogue about self-care and making yourself a priority. Take particular note of anything you would like to include more in your life.

Rate the following areas according to how well you think you are doing:

3 = *I do this well* (e.g., frequently)

2 = *I do this OK* (e.g., occasionally)

1 = *I barely or rarely do this*

0 = *I never do this*

? = *This never occurred to me*

Physical self-care

____ Eat regularly (e.g., breakfast, lunch, and dinner)

____ Eat healthily

____ Exercise

____ Get regular medical care for prevention

____ Get medical care when needed

____ Take time off when sick

____ Get massages

____ Dance, swim, walk, run, play sports, sing, or do some other fun physical activity

____ Take time to be sexual — with myself, with a partner

____ Get enough sleep

____ Wear clothes I like

____ Take vacations

____ Take day trips or mini-vacations

____ Make time away from telephones

____ Other:

Psychological self-care

____ Make time for self-reflection

____ Notice my inner experience — listen to my thoughts, beliefs, attitudes, feelings

____ Have my own personal psychotherapy

____ Write in a journal

____ Read literature that is unrelated to work

____ Do something at which I am not expert or in charge

____ Attend to minimising stress in my life

____ Engage my intelligence in a new area — for example, go to an art show, sports event, theatre

____ Receive from others

____ Be curious

____ Say no to extra responsibilities sometimes

____ Other:

Emotional self-care

____ Spend time with others whose company I enjoy

____ Stay in contact with important people in my life

____ Give myself affirmations, praise myself

____ Love myself

____ Reread favourite books, re-view favourite movies

____ Identify comforting activities, objects, people, places and seek them out

____ Allow myself to cry

____ Find things that make me laugh

____ Express my outrage in social action, letters, donations, marches, protests

____ Other:

Spiritual self-care

____ Make time for reflection

____ Spend time in nature

____ Find a spiritual connection or community

____ Be open to inspiration

____ Cherish my optimism and hope

____ Be aware of non-material aspects of life

____ Try at times not to be in charge or the expert

____ Be open to not knowing

____ Identify what is meaningful to me and notice its place in my life

____ Meditate

____ Pray

____ Sing

____ Have experiences of awe

____ Contribute to causes in which you believe

____ Read inspirational literature or listen to inspirational talks, music

____ Other:

Workplace or professional self-care

____ Take a break during the workday (e.g., lunch)

____ Take time to chat with co-workers

____ Make quiet time to complete tasks

____ Identify projects or tasks that are exciting and rewarding

____ Set limits with clients and colleagues

____ Arrange work space so it is comfortable and comforting

____ Get regular supervision or consultation

____ Negotiate for my needs (benefits, pay rise)

____ Have a peer support group

____ Balance within my work-life and workday

Overall balance

____ Balance among work, family, relationships, play, and rest

Chapter 6: Review questions

1. Define vicarious trauma in your own words: what does it mean to you?
2. List some of the causes of vicarious trauma?
3. Considering the individual level approach to minimising vicarious trauma, think of three strategies that you can implement?
4. What methods of organisational-care exist within your workplace in order to prevent burnout among staff?
5. As a professional do you feel that you maintain realistic expectations of yourself and others? What can you do to ensure you create reasonable, achievable goals?

References

Abdulrehman, R.Y., & De Luca, R.V. (2001). The implications of childhood sexual abuse on adult social behaviour. *Journal of Family Violence, 16*(2), 1573–2851.

Alaggia, R. (2005). Disclosing the trauma of child sexual abuse: A gender analysis. *Journal of Loss and Trauma, 10,* 453–470.

Alaggia, R., & Kirshenbaum, S. (2005). Speaking the unspeakable: Exploring the impact of family dynamics on child sexual abuse disclosures. *Families in Society, 86,* 227–234.

Australian Bureau of Statistics. (2007). *Criminal courts 2005–2006.* Canberra, Australia: Author.

Australian Bureau of Statistics. (2009). *Reported crime victims.* Canberra, Australia: Author.

Australian Institute of Health and Welfare. (2002). *Child Protection Australia 2000–2001* (Child Welfare Series No. 29). Canberra, Australia: Author.

Bayliss, M. (2008). *The cost of caring; vicarious trauma, compassion fatigue, burn out.* Retrieved from http://www.imaginif.com.au/the-cost-of-caring-vicarious-trauma-compassion-fatigue-burn-out/

Beitchman, J.H., Zucker, K.J., Hood, J.E., DaCosta, D., & Akaman D. (1991) A review of the short-term effects of child sexual abuse. *Journal of Abuse and Neglect, 15,* 537–556.

Beitchman, J.H., Zucker, K.J., Hood, J.E., DaCosta, D., Akaman D. & Cassavia, E. (1992) A review of the long-term effects of child sexual abuse. *Child Abuse and Neglect, 16,* 101–118.

Bell, H., Kulkarni, S., & Dalton, L. (2003). Organizational prevention of vicarious trauma. *Families in Society: The Journal of Contemporary Human Services, 84*(4), 463–470.

Bhave, S., & Mashanker, V. (2006). Sexual abuse in children and adolescents. In S. Gupte (Ed.), *Recent advances in pediatrics* (Special Volume 17, pp. 268–290). Daryaganj, India: Jaypee Brothers Medical Publishers.

Briggs, F. (1995). *From victim to offender: How child sexual abuse victims become offenders.* Sydney, Australia: Allen & Unwin.

Briere, J., & Elliott, D. (1994). Immediate and long-term impacts of child sexual abuse. *The Future of Children, 4*(2), 54–69.

Browne, K., & Lynch, M. (1994). Prevention: Actions speak louder than words. *Child Abuse Review, 3,* 241–244.

Bureau of Justice Statistics. (2000). Sexual assault of young children as reported to law enforcement: Victim, incident, and offender characteristics. Washington, DC: Us Department of Justice.

Caffaro-Rouget, A., Lang, R.A.. & Van Santen, V. (1989). The impact of child sexual abuse on victims' adjustment. *Sexual Abuse: A Journal of Research and Treatment, 2,* 29–47.

Core Sex Offender Management and Intervention Program. (2001). *The Offence Cycle. Management and Intervention Program.* Victoria, Australia: Author.

Crisci, G., Lay, M., & Lowenstein, L. (1998). *Paper dolls and paper airplanes: therapeutic exercises for sexually traumatized children.* Toronto: Champion Press.

Crisma, M., Bascelli, E., Paci, D., & Romito, R. (2004). Adolescents who experienced sexual abuse: Fears, needs and impediments to disclosure. *Child Abuse & Neglect, 28,* 1035–1048.

Denov, M.S. (2003). To a safer place? Victims of sexual abuse by females and their disclosures to professionals. *Child Abuse and Neglect, 27*, 47–61.

Department of Child Safety. (2007). *Child Protection Queensland 2005–2006 performance report.* Brisbane, Australia: Author.

Department of Community Services. (2006). *Spotlight on safety: Community attitudes to child protection, foster care and parenting.* Sydney, Australia: Author.

Dympna House. (1998). *Info kit: A booklet on childhood sexual abuse.* Sydney, Australia: Dympna House.

Elliot, A., & Carnes, C. (2001). Reactions of nonoffending parents to the sexual abuse of their child: A review of the literature. *Child Maltreatment, 6*(4), 314–331.

Finkelhor, D. (1984). *Child sexual abuse: New theory and research.* New York:The Free Press.

Finkelhor, D. (1994). The international epidemiology of child sexual abuse. *Child Abuse and Neglect, 18*, 409–417.

Fitzgerald, J. (2006). *The attrition of sexual offences from the New South Wales Criminal Justice System.* Sydney, Australia: NSW Bureau of Crime Statistics & Research, 2006.

Gilbert, R., Spatz-Widom, C., Browne, K., Fergusson, D., Webb, E., & Janson, S. (2009). Burden and consequences of child maltreatment in high income countries. *The Lancet, 373*(9657), 68–81.

Gil, E. (1991). *Healing power of play: Working with abused children.* New York: Guilford Publications.

Goldman, J., & Padayachi. (1997). The prevalence and nature of child sexual abuse in Queensland, Australia. *Child Abuse Neglect, 21*, 489–498.

Goodman-Brown, T.B., Edelstein, R.S., Goodman, G.S., Jones, G.P.H., & Gordon, D.S. (2003). Why children tell: A model of children's disclosure of sexual abuse. *Child Abuse and Neglect, 27*, 525–540.

Hansard. (2002). Commonwealth Senator Andrew Murray, June 19.

Hanson, R.K., Gordon, A., Harris, A.J.R., Marques, J.K., Murphy, W., Quinsey, V.L., & Seto, M.C. (2002). First report of the collaborative outcome data project on the effectiveness of psychological treatment for sex offenders. *Sexual Abuse: A Journal of Research and Treatment, 14*(2), 169–194.

Hoy, A., & Bright, D.A. (in press). Effectiveness of a Sex Offender Treatment Programme: A risk band analysis. Sydney.

James, M. (2000). *Child abuse and neglect: Redefining the issues* (Trends and Issues Series, No. 146). Canberra, Australia: Australian Institute of Criminology.

Jensen, T.K., Gulbrandsen, W., Mossige, S., Reichelt, S., & Tjersland, O.A. (2005). Reporting possible sexual abuse: A qualitative study on children's perspectives and the context for disclosure. *Child Abuse and Neglect, 29*(12), 1395–1413.

Kogan, S.M. (2004). Disclosing unwanted sexual experiences: Results from a national survey of adolescent women. *Child Abuse and Neglect, 28*, 147–165.

Lanning, K. (2001). Child molesters and cyber paedophiles: A behavioural perspective. In R. Hazelwood & A. Burgess (Eds.), *Practical aspects of rape investigation* (3rd ed., pp. 199–220). Boca Raton, FL: CRC Press.

Leclerc, B., Proulx, J., & McKibben, A. (2005). Modus operandi of sexual offenders working or doing voluntary work with children and adolescents. *Journal of Sexual Aggression, 11*(2), 187–195.

Losel, F., & Schmucker, M. (2005). The effectiveness of treatment for sexual offenders. A comprehensive analysis. *Journal of Experimental Criminology, 1*, 117–146.

Mamun, A., Lawlor, D., O'Calloghan, M., Bor, W., Williams, G., & Najman, J. (2007). Does childhood sexual abuse predict young adult's BMI? A birth cohort study. Obesity, 15(8): 2103–2110.

Morrison, Z. (2007). *'Feeling heavy': Vicarious trauma and other issues facing those who work in the sexual assault field* (Australian Centre for the Study of Sexual Assault [ACSSA] Wrap, 4) Melbourne, Australia: Australian Institute of Family Studies.

National Child Protection Clearinghouse. (2005). *Child abuse prevention resource sheet* (No .7) Melbourne, Australia: Australian Institute of Family Studies.

O'Connor, K.J., & Braverman, L.M.C. (Eds.). (1997). *Play therapy theory and practice: A comparative presentation.* John Wiley & Sons.

Orsoli, L., Kia-Keating, M., & Grossman, F.K. (2008). 'I keep that hush-hush': Male survivors of sexual abuse and the challenges of disclosure. *Journal of Counselling Psychology, 55*(3), 333–345.

Paine, M.L., & Hansen, D.J. (2002). Factors influencing children to self-disclose sexual abuse. *Clinical Psychology Review, 22*, 271–295.

Pearlman, L.A., & Saakvitne, K.W. (1995). *Trauma and the therapist: Counter transference and vicarious traumatisation in psychotherapy with incest survivors.* New York: Norton.

Queensland Crime Commission. (2000). *Project Axis: Volume 1.* Brisbane, Australia: Author.

Queensland Crime and Misconduct Commission. (2003). *Seeking justice: An inquiry into the handling of sexual offences by the criminal justice system.* Brisbane, Australia: Author.

Queensland Criminal Justice Commission. (1999). *Reported sexual offences in Queensland.* Brisbane, Australia: Author.

Smallbone, S., & Wortley, R. (2000). *Child sexual abuse in Queensland: Offender characteristics and modus operandi.* Brisbane, Australia: Queensland Crime Commission.

Smith, D.W., Letourneau, E.J., Saunders B.E., Kilpatrick, D.G, Resnick, H.S., & Best, C.L. (2000). Delay in disclosure of childhood rape: Results from a national survey. *Child Abuse and Neglect, 24*(2), 273–287.

Spataro, J., Mullen, P., Burgess, P., Wells, D., & Mos, S. (2004). Impact of child sexual abuse on mental health: Prospective study in males and females. *British Journal of Psychiatry, 184*, 416–421.

Spatz-Widom, C. (1993). *The Cycle of Violence.* Paper presented at the Second Conference on Violence (Australian Institute of Criminology, June).

Wasco, S.M., Campbell, R., & Clark, M. (2002). A multiple case stud of rape victims advocates' self-care routines: The influence of organisational context. *American Journal of Community Psychology, 30*(5), 731–760.

Watson, B. (2007). *Sexual abuse of girls and adult couple relationships: Risk and protective factors.* Thesis submitted for degree of Doctor of Philosophy, School of Psychology, Griffith University, Australia.

Wyatt, G.E., & Mickey, M.R. (1987). Ameliorating the effects of child sexual abuse: an exploratory study of support by parents and others. *Journal of Interpersonal Violence, 2*, 403–414.

Self-Evaluation Tool

This evaluation focuses on how you will transfer your learnings to your own workplace setting. It is designed primarily for you to critically assess your strengths and skills you feel may require further development; and to develop an action plan for transferring your newfound skills and knowledge to your professional practice.

The aim is to assist you to possess a better understanding of your strengths in working with children and young people who have experienced sexual assault, be more self-aware of areas where you may require further support and/or training, and develop an action plan for applying this new knowledge and skills to your workplace setting.

---

1. Has this book increased my level of confidence, knowledge and skills?

2. What are some of the new strengths/therapeutic skills I now have to support children and young people who have experienced sexual assault?

3a. Are there any gaps in my knowledge/skills that I feel require further development in regards to working with this client group?

3b. How will I go about developing these skills further?

4. How will I transfer my learnings from this book to my workplace setting?

Feedback Form

We would like to ensure that our resources meet your needs and welcome any feedback you have on the Bravehearts' Toolbox for Practitioners. Please photocopy this page and fax/email or post to the address below.

Please rate on a scale of 1-5 (1 being Poor and 5 being Excellent):

Rating

1. Value of the information in relation to my job/workplace ______
2. Usefulness of the activities outlined ______
3. The activities were easy to follow ______

Please answer the following questions:

4. Are there any extra topics or information that you think could be included in the Toolbox?

____

____

____

5. What aspect of the Toolbox did you find the most useful?

____

____

____

6. What aspect of the Toolbox did you find the least useful?

____

____

____

7. Please feel free to make any other comments …

____

____

____

Thank you for providing your feedback! Please forward to:
Carol Ronken, Research Manager, Bravehearts Inc.
PO Box 575, Arundel BC QLD 4214 Australia.
E-mail: research@bravehearts.org.au Fax: 07 5552 3088

Lightning Source UK Ltd.
Milton Keynes UK
UKHW032254260220
359393UK00004B/162

9 781921 513886